This edition of Henry Miller's HAMLET LETTERS is of imponderable importance to anyone who pretends to know and admire (or hate) what is without doubt some of the greatest prose in our current language. It has been edited by one of these very people, as is obvious from the first word in Michael Hargraves' introduction. His reverence for Miller is as natural as Miller himself is supernatural.

--M.F.K. Fisher

Other Henry Miller Books from Capra Press:

SEXTET: The Collected Chapbooks (1977)
THE WORLD OF LAWRENCE (1980)
REFLECTIONS (Edited by Twinka Thiebaud) (1981)
THE PAINTINGS OF HENRY MILLER (1982)
BOOK OF FRIENDS: A Trilogy (1987)

Henry Miller and Michael Fraenkel
Louveciennes, ca. 1931

HENRY MILLER'S HAMLET LETTERS

Edited, and with an Historical Introduction
by Michael Hargraves
and an Original Preface by Henry Miller

CAPRA PRESS
SANTA BARBARA

Henry Miller Preface copyright ©1981 by Michael Hargraves
Abridged edition copyright ©1988 by Michael Hargraves
FIRST AMERICAN EDITION

Cover design by Maureen Luran
Designed and typeset in Garamond by Jim Cook, Santa Barbara, California

Library of Congress Publication Data:
Miller, Henry (1891-1980) Henry Miller's Hamlet Letters
    1. Miller, Henry, 1891-1980—Correspondence   2. Hargraves, Michael (1952-)
Abridgement of Hamlet as first published in 2 v. in 1939-1941.

Published by CAPRA PRESS
Post Office Box 2068
Santa Barbara, California 93120

EDITOR'S FOREWORD

For most readers, save for the most inveterate Henry Miller enthusiast or collector, this work will be essentially new and unknown.

This Paris-written work is primarily unknown due to the small limitation of the copies printed, the lack of distribution, how it was printed (on variable paper stocks, bound in paper wrappers) and where it was originally published (Puerto Rico and Mexico.)

The work was originally entitled *Hamlet* and at the time was something of an experimental literary venture: an epistolary, improvisational collaboration between Miller and Michael Fraenkel, an obscure Lithuanian-born American writer. (Their mutual friend Alfred Perles was in at the genesis of the project but soon dropped out and none of his letters were ever published.) The book's theme was to be Shakespeare's *Hamlet* and was to last a total of 1,000 pages, not one more, not one less. However, it didn't happen.

Before going on about the mechanics of the book, I think it's important to give a brief history of the *Hamlet* letters as well as how this edition came into being:

The actual correspondence took place from November 1935 until October 1938. With few exceptions the letters were written in Paris. (The genesis of this project took place at the Cafe Zeyer in Paris on the terrace, which by the way I visited during the editing of the book—it no longer has a terrace and Miller certainly wouldn't have

5

been able to afford to drink there with his then penurious situation under the new chic regime.)

Under the Carrefour imprint, Fraenkel published Volume One at Santruce, Puerto Rico, in June 1939. The volume was incomplete, lacking some 100 pages of letters. It was printed in Belgium in an edition of 500 copies.

Volume Two came out in June 1941, in Mexico, also in an edition of 500 copies (although there is said to be 20 special copies, bound in full red morocco, signed by both Miller and Fraenkel, as well.)

A complete edition of Volume One was published in July 1943, also from Mexico in an edition of 500 copies.

A French edition was issued in February 1956 by Correa/Buchet & Chastel in Paris. It was an abridgement of both writer's letters by about one-third for a one-volume edition. The most complete version of the letters was printed by Fraenkel's widow, Daphne at London in 1962, again under the Carrefour imprint. It contained a few pen drawings and photographs and was bound in Japanese-style paper wrappers with red ribbon, again in an edition of 500 copies (printed in letterpress, no less!)

This Capra Press edition marks the first official American printing. And the effort to get it published was by no means an easy feat.

I first encountered the book at a library when I moved to California in 1975. Not being able to check it out (it was classified as a rare book!), I had to read it in one sitting, some 400 pages worth. I was greatly impressed with what I'd read, especially Miller's passages. I felt then and still do that it contains some of Miller's best writing, some of his freest yet provocative thoughts on paper, and instilled with the wry, wonderfully vulgar Miller I'd read previously. (One must remember that this book was being composed just after *Tropic of Cancer* and during the writing of *Tropic of Capricorn.*) Other readers of Miller I've spoken with over the years agree with my enthusiasm of the book.

I wondered why the book was unavailable in America at the time but didn't discover the reason until I went to Europe for the second time.

During that stay I made a brief visit to London where I found a copy of the 1962 edition in a used bookshop. I learned from the bookseller that Mrs. Michael Fraenkel was alive and living in London. Happily, I located her and asked her many questions regarding the book. She told me she'd originally decided to reprint the book as a tribute of her late husband, told me of her dislike of Henry Miller and that the fiftieth anniversary of the Carrefour Press was soon to be celebrated.

Naive as to what I was about to get into, I suggested that she allow me to find an American publisher for the book. When I returned to California, I began a long term correspondence with Daphne Fraenkel concerning *Hamlet*'s future in the States. I was offered the American publication rights and went forth in finding a publisher.

During this period I met and became friends with Henry Miller, then living in Pacific Palisades, California. At our first meeting I brought along my copy of Daphne's edition which he inscribed for me—"To Michael Hargraves—the proud possessor of an unauthorized edition by me." Miller had reciprocal feelings toward Mrs. Fraenkel. Afterward, when we began a correspondence on the *Hamlet* book, Miller let it be known further his dislike for her. In one letter to me he wrote, "My feeling about Daphne hasn't changed over the years. I always regarded her as a rather astute horse's ass." While in another letter wrote: "She cheated me out of royalties on that handsome British edition. More, she treated me in her blurbs as if I were the fifth wheel on a wagon." (The blurbs Miller refers to are on the back wrapper of the book taken from a few contemporary reviews of the 1940s.)

Miller's hatred of Daphne Fraenkel stemmed primarily from not being able to get the book published in the United States (as well as Fraenkel not giving him any rights to the book at the time it was first published.) It was a case of anger and jealousy, and Miller's feelings were rightly hurt.

While some attempts were made previously to issue the book in America, nothing ever came of it, mainly due to Mrs. Fraenkel's resistance. There has been, however, some question in regards to the copyright of the *Hamlet* book. Elmer Gertz, Miller's trial lawyer for *Tropic of Cancer,* claims the book was never copyrighted. Subsequent investigation through the U.S. Copyright Office has proven that the book was indeed never copyrighted but that copies were deposited there, presumably by Fraenkel. If Fraenkel did indeed copyright the book, he most certainly failed to renew it, thus making it part of the public domain.

The process of finding a publisher began and the road to success was a rather bumpy affair. To help in the matter, Miller wrote an original preface for the new edition (which appears here) gratis in gratitude for my attempting to get the book published in America. For a period of some two years, I approached practically every major, minor and university press with the book. (Even Capra Press couldn't financially tackle the 400-some-odd-page book; New Directions and Grove Press, Henry's old publishers, didn't want to tackle it as I was obliged at the time to publish the book in toto.)

As a last ditch effort, in hopes of getting a grant to publish the book myself or generate some enthusiasm from another source, I published a small book entitled *The Hamlet Additions: The Unpublishing of the Henry Miller-Michael Fraenkel Book of Correspondence Called Hamlet* in 1981 in an edition of 200 copies. I solicited essays from Norman Mailer, Alfred Perles, Robert Gover and Alain Robbe-Grillet which were gladly written by these admirers of Miller. Alas, that too failed to get the book back into print.

Aside from the voluminous size problem, another problem with getting publishers interested was the general obscurity of Michael Fraenkel. My own knowledge of Fraenkel was limited to his *Bastard Death, The Genesis of The Tropic of Cancer* and of course his part of the *Hamlet* book. It has been written that Fraenkel was just as obscure a writer at the time of his death in 1957 as he was during whatever literary heights there may have been during his lifetime.

I draw the reader to a fine study of Fraenkel by Walter Lowenfels (a good friend of both Miller and Fraenkel) and Howard McCord entitled *The Life of Fraenkel's Death* (Washington State University Press, 1970). It's a good introduction to Fraenkel and many important facts are pointed out concerning the relationship between Fraenkel and Miller.

For example, Lowenfels and McCord are essentially correct when they point out Miller's lack of credit to Fraenkel as an inspirational part of his creative writing process. It was Fraenkel who introduced him to some of his life-long friends as well as introducing him to some important books that were to become so meaningful to Miller. Fraenkel, who by the way was the model for the "Boris" character in *Tropic of Cancer,* was indeed a very intelligent man whose contrary style flamed Miller's thoughts throughout that early Paris period right through the completion of the *Hamlet* book. It's been said that Miller had little to do with Fraenkel after 1938 (although Miller wrote a brief tribute of sorts on Fraenkel for the now-famous Gotham Book Mart catalogue "We Moderns" in 1940.) This probably is due mostly in Fraenkel's denial to Miller for getting their mutual venture reprinted.

The reviewers of the day were somewhat flummoxed by the two writer's efforts. Only a handful of small reviews plus The New Republic made mention of the book, either of one volume or the other. Apparently Fraenkel was lax in getting out review copies or the bigger publications didn't deem it worthy of space. Although Miller conceded to me he thought the book as a whole was "a white elephant" and "a joke," he nonetheless felt passionate about what he wrote in the process, feeling it contained some of his clearest thoughts as well as some of his more substantial in content.

Lawrence Durrell years later said of the *Hamlet* Letters that it was "another book which is exasperatingly good in some parts, exasperatingly bad in others."

While Hamlet is indeed the focal point of the book, and almost always the recurring bridgehead both writers come back to, the book is effectively a book of philosophy, two distinct ones, of Miller and Fraenkel, of life and death. The beauty of the book lies not in the discussion of Hamlet (although I'm quite sure the Shakespearean scholar could have a royal field day with the book), but of the tangents the two writers go off into to reveal themselves. It is the "side-tracking" that lets the writers flow, allowing for free-form discussions of many things close to their hearts and of the world at large. Fraenkel claims in his last letter to Miller that "you have broken all the rules of the game." That is precisely correct and precisely why Miller's come off the best. When Miller got rolling on something he felt passionate about he would explode like a rocket on the launching pad, thrusting upwards, rising higher and higher until all the fuel of his thoughts were exhausted. In this situation, Miller was fueled by Fraenkel's thoughts, anger and defensiveness. Miller seems to fly higher into the atmosphere with each passing letter.

The reason of making this edition a strictly Henry Miller book rather than an edited version of the two men's letters as the French did (and failed in doing so) is due mostly to the size of the book and Fraenkel's obscurity to the reading public. Although the purist in me would have preferred a complete edition of the book (perhaps the success of this selection will allow for a companion volume of Fraenkel's letters), the Miller letters stand alone as an interesting book. What should be understood, however, is that there is no complete *Hamlet* book in any edition. Letters over the years from the time Fraenkel first published the book were either lost in part or whole or not considered for inclusion for whatever reason. So, the reader need not feel cheated by any means.

Of the twenty-two letters by Miller which appear in the most complete edition of *Hamlet*, this abridged edition contains twenty of them, all edited to some extent. What's been edited out for the most part are salutation and closing remarks, dates of the letters, obscure personal references between the two writers which Miller replies to, many comments Miller makes about Fraenkel's book *Bastard Death* and many quotes from other books, especially in foreign languages.

The letters are segregated only by number, being kept in chronological order.

Some of Miller's retorts reacting from the previous Fraenkel letter have been retained in order to depict Miller's sense of humor or general state-of-mind at the time in which he composed his letter. Although in some cases these quips won't make complete sense, their inclusion shouldn't muddle the flow of the work with any real danger.

Many of the topics Miller touches upon in his letters are those in which he later commented on with his return to America. Of course his ubiquitous feeling of vileness and ugliness for America is peppered throughout the work. One must remember that when these letters were being composed he believed he'd never return here and could vent his anger to his heart's content. He also talks about his affinity with the Chinese, of their sages and philosophies. In one letter, Miller gives us his impressions of Aldous Huxley, a writer with whom in other writings has indicated he admires. In a most profound letter, Miller expounds on his theory of color. It is an amazing letter, one in which truly impressed Fraenkel resulting with a glowing positive response.

Other matters Miller touches upon include schizophrenia, the numerous writers, painters and musicians who had inspired him, the movies, the Jews and their life styles and thoughts, and his thoughts on fiction as art. Mainly, as I've stated before, this is a book of Miller's philosophy. Weaved throughout the way station of *Hamlet*, Miller depicts himself as a man full of life, a man who enjoyed himself and lived fully as opposed to Fraenkel's death wish philosophical approach to the rites of life. Miller, as well as Fraenkel, knew the world was doomed, was "dead." It is still doomed and dying, however, Miller possessed the same feeling as Baudelaire, that being, doomed to hope. Miller never gave up, even at his bleakest moment. Thus the title of this edition could have been called *When One Has Life He Will Know How to Guard It,* which comes from the last sentence of his last letter.

This book should surprise and impress the Henry Miller reader and, with luck, will do so as well as for the new readers. Not only that, it'll probably never make Shakespeare's *Hamlet* the same again.

—MICHAEL HARGRAVES
Paris-Los Angeles
July 4, 1986—May 18, 1988

PREFACE

I met Michael Fraenkel in the early days of my sojourn in Paris. I was penniless, begging meals, sleeping wherever I could; in short, I was thoroughly down and out. I believe I met him through Bertha Schrank with whom I was then in love. She probably told him that I was a writer and in desperate need. He was relatively well off, having recently returned from the Philippines where he sold a quantity of books which Doubleday had remaindered. He was playing the stock market and doing quite well for himself. He too was a writer, I soon found out. He had written one book—*Werther's Younger Brother*, influenced by Goethe's *Sorrows of Werther*. If I remember rightly he was already living in the Villa Seurat at No. 18. He allowed me to sleep on the floor a few nights. There was no extra bed or couch available. I was damn glad to have a roof over my head.

And so it began.

The day the *Tropic of Cancer* came out I found myself living in 18 Villa Seurat. Who should occupy the ground floor *(rez-de-chaussee)* but Michael Fraenkel. I was under the impression he owned the building, but before I went to Greece it was owned by a Madame Guisbourg.

Soon Fraenkel was visiting me daily. Often he would arrive in time for breakfast, stay for lunch and dinner, and return to his abode toward midnight. All day and night we were talking, talking, talking.

I suppose he would have referred to these talks as discussions. To me they were anything but discussions. Though I seemed to get nothing from them I was fascinated, and exhausted at the end of each day. Two people could hardly be more unalike than Fraenkel and myself. He had what you could call a "rabbinical" mind, which meant sharp as a razor blade. Furthermore, it never wore out from use. As for myself, I must have been a pretty good talker too. But I had never encountered such a one as Fraenkel. Talk was his meat. He simply could not utter a plain, declarative sentence. Everything he said seemed provocative to me. My friend Perles never participated in these talks except when we were desperate for cash. Then the two of us would call on him in his apartment downstairs and while engaging him in heated argument about any old thing proceed to filch some bank notes from his wallet.

After a few months of this talky-talk business one day at the Cafe Zeyer, Place d'Orleans, Fraenkel suggested that we write each other letters instead of talking.

"On what theme?" I asked.

"Oh, anything and everything," I believe he replied. "And what about a title for the letters?"

He smiled, that peculiarly sardonic smile he could so easily summon, and began to reel off possible titles. They were all far from the mark—he didn't seem to care much what the title should be. What he was concerned about was that it must be exactly 1,000 pages long. "At page 1,000," he added, "we must stop even if it's in the middle of a sentence."

Before we quit the cafe that afternoon we had agreed that the title for the book should be "Hamlet." (We almost had decided on "The Merry Widow Waltz.")

I forgot to say that from the start Fraenkel made it clear that he would publish the book, at his expense. I was to split royalties with him. To my surprise I discovered that he owned a small press somewhere in Belgium. (I believe that originally he and Walter Lowenfels, the poet, had established it together.)

Well, we didn't quite make page 1,000 when we quit writing the Hamlet letters. I think I had become a little too insulting in my letters to him. Certainly by this time we were no longer the best of friends, if ever we had been.

Naturally the book received a poor reception. A French publisher (Buchet/Chastel) published it in translation but in doing so, deleted a goodly portion of the letters, very much in the manner of the Japanese. But the French edition fared no better than the English one.

Some years later, after Fraenkel's death, his widow Daphne Moschos who had inherited the rights to the book, brought out a British edition for which I never received a copy of the book nor a penny in royalties. Just recently she sold her copyright to an American fan of mine, Michael Hargraves, who is responsible for the appearance of this American edition.

Looking back upon our venture almost fifty years later it seems to me that it was a sort of bowling game we played. That is to say he would set up the pins and I would knock them down as best I could.

—Henry Miller
2/19/79

I

Last night I was sitting at Ecole-Militaire. It was All Saints Day. I had just come from a walk through the Rue Saint-Dominique, a walk deliberately undertaken because I wanted to reexperience certain emotions. I experienced exactly what I had hoped to recapture and, seating myself on the terrasse of a cafe I digested my emotions. And then I began to think about *Hamlet.* I thought how perverse it was to be thinking about *Hamlet* on a day like this, All Souls Day in France, when the most disgusting specimens of bourgeois French vegetable life take possession of the street. I thought that not a Frenchman alive could possibly understand the chaos of my thoughts. There they were, all flitting about me in somber black raiment, and absolutely impervious not only to *Hamlet* but to the whole Anglo-Saxon world out of which *Hamlet* sprang. If Hamlet, as I thought, was the arch symbol of death-in-life, then what were they, these phantoms brushing by me? Life and bastard life. In which case Hamlet is life and this but a bastard life. Yet these people are active; each one has a goal, a purpose, a direction. This is not the activity of the German or the American. This is *French* life, than which nothing is more satisfactory and nothing more empty. How then *Hamlet? Why Hamlet? Hamlet* is the drama of the northern soul, a drama which takes place outside the confines of that reality which the French call life.

How strange it is, I think to myself, that here we are in France, and none of us French. We sit at the Cafe Zeyer and we decide to write this book. It is not a book that the French will like. It is not a book for our American compatriots either. Yet this book is born of France and of America. Born in a moment of extreme lassitude, born out of a despair created by the inertia and paralysis surrounding us.

Sitting at Ecole-Militaire I try to recall the story of *Hamlet* as Shakespeare gave it to us. There was a sickly Dane of poetic cast who could not act. He makes a famous speech about suicide—"to be or not to be"—which seems to have made a profound impression upon the world. In the end he dies, and with him a number of other people. We are left with his doubts, his ruminations. By an almost unanimous verdict it was one of the best plays which Shakespeare wrote.

Such is the play. The effect is something else, something out of all proportion to the play, even if it *were* the greatest play ever written, which it isn't. Why then *Hamlet*, which is so firmly lodged in our consciousness that only when our whole Western civilization is wiped out will it disappear? It seems to me that the answer to this lies in the very enthusiasm with which we agreed to undertake this task. Hamlet is in our bowels. That very will which is aborted, that chaos, that yearning for a beyond which distinguishes us from the French, that is what rumbles eternally in our blood and leads us on to a defeat at the hands of life. There were plenty of Hamlets before Shakespeare. But with Shakespeare the true Hamlet comes to fruition. It comes at the height of the Renaissance. It springs out of the third eye.

In referring to the *Oedipus* of Sophocles Nietzsche tries to explain to us that the purpose of the drama was to show that "the noble man does not sin." "All laws," he adds, "all natural order, yea, the moral world itself may be destroyed through his action, but through this very action a higher magic circle of influences is brought into play, with which a new world on the ruins of the old that has been overthrown." There in a nutshell you have the difference between the ancient world, at its heyday, and the modern world of Hamlet. *The noble man does not sin*, says Nietzsche. Not until we come to Rimbaud do we have a feeble echo of this. Feeble, I say, because in Rimbaud the sense of guilt is atrophied, not conquered. And here again we mark the gulf which separates the modern world from the ancient world of the Greeks. *Oedipus* is the supreme drama of guilt. It establishes forever the divine innocence of man. Whereas Hamlet, the supreme drama of doubt, is loaded with the guilt of two thousand years of ignominious suffering, the very symbol of the modern man's inner bankruptcy.

Let me revert for a moment to the circumstances which surround (for the condition has not altered since) the conception of this, *our* Hamlet. Originally our idea was to take a badly written story by some celebrity and rewrite it in *our* fashion. We wanted a story that everybody would recognize, whose title alone was sufficient. And after a few days of vainly racking our brains we came to the conclusion that it would scarcely be worth the pains, assuming we *could* find an appropriate theme. And so, inevitably, we came to a choice between *The Merry Widow* and *Hamlet*. How modern! That there should be no supreme difference between a *Hamlet* and a *Merry Widow!* And not only this, I beg you to observe, but further ... was it not the fact that we suddenly agreed to write a thousand pages, not one more, not one less, which clinched the idea? Where was Hamlet then? The thousand pages were more important than *Hamlet* itself. *Hamlet*, that is to say, hath neither beginning nor end. The whole world has become *Hamlet* and what we say will neither add nor subtract from the subject.

This is Hamlet! If there is to be any success in our endeavor it will be in laying the ghost. For Hamlet still stalks the streets. The fault is not Shakespeare's—the fault is ours. None of us have become naturally modern enough to waylay this ghost and strangle it. For the ghost is not the father which was murdered, nor the conscience which was uneasy, but the time-spirit which has been creaking like a rusty pendulum. In this book it should be our high purpose to set the pendulum swinging smoothly again so that we synchronize with past and future. Are the times out of joint? Then look to the clock! Not the clock on the mantelpiece, but the chronometer inside which tells when you are living and when you are not. I should say blandly—throw away all existent clocks! We don't want to know what time it is by sun or moon, but by past and future. Now we are swamped with time—Western Union time, Eastern Standard time, Greenwich time, sidereal time, Einsteinian time, reading time, bedtime, all kinds of time which tell us nothing about what is passing inside us, or even outside us. We are moving on the escalator of time . . .

In winding up this salutation I notice that the calendar says *November 7th!* I just want to point out to you how false and unreliable the calendar is, because according to my chronology it is still November 2nd and I have not moved an inch from the terrasse at Ecole-Militaire. It may be that everything I have to say will be written from this terrasse which is particularly pleasant and soothing to the senses.

2

It's very good of you to give me such explicit answers. Only, my feeling is that you are trying to muddle me. You seem to take for granted that I have the utmost confidence in your "erudition," that I will take what you say about Hamlet on faith. You are mistaken here, in two ways. First, I distrust all erudition, yours included. Secondly, your letter contains no erudition. If I ask you a few simple and direct questions it's in order to know what *you* think, and not what you have learned others think about Hamlet. No, I did not want the low-down on Hamlet, as you pretend to give it to me, but a simple statement of your own reactions. But perhaps this is your Hamlet-like way of answering questions. I suspect you of padding the book . . .

Just the same, your answers provoke me into giving you a little clearer picture of *my* impression of Hamlet, for, as I explained to you previously, the original Hamlet (meaning in this instance Shakespeare's *Hamlet*) is now swallowed up in the universal Hamlet. Whatever Shakespeare had to say is now irrelevant and thoroughly unimportant, except as a basis of departure. However weak may have been Prince Alfred's thesis about "objectivity," nevertheless the same criticism of Shakespeare registers itself in my mind—that he was a puppet-master. And in my case I make bold to add recklessness to ignorance by stating that it was only because of this puppet show quality in Shakespeare that his works have had such a universal appeal. This universal appeal, like the Bible's, I must add parenthetically, is based on faith and non-investigation. People simply do not read Shakespeare any more, nor the Bible either. They read *about* Shakespeare. The critical literature built up about his name and works is vastly more fruitful and stimulating than Shakespeare himself, about whom nobody seems to know very much, his very identify being a mystery. This, I want to point out to you, is not true about other writers of the past, notably Petronius, Boccaccio, Rabelais, Dante, Villon, etc. It is true of Homer, Virgil, Torquato Tasso, Spinoza, etc. Hugo, the great French God, is read only by adolescents today, and *ought* only to be read by them. Shakespeare, the English god, is also read today mostly by adolescents—compulsory reading. When you pick him up later in life you find it almost impossible to overcome the prejudice established against him by the schoolmasters, by their way of presenting him. Shakespeare was just the pompous, flatulent sort of giant whom the English *would* convert into a sacred bull. Lacking depth they gave him girth and a girth that ill conceals the stuffed pillows.

But as I say, I want to give you a little more of my own recollection of *Hamlet*, rather confused, it is true, but honest. I don't doubt that if a questionnaire were sent around the English-speaking world there would be still more confusion about the subject. To begin with, I dismiss the first reading, which was compulsory and, absolutely nil in results. (Except for a detestation of the subject which over a period of years has gradually changed into an archaeological curiosity, so to speak.) I mean by this that today I am much more interested in hearing what Mr. X . . . has to say about Hamlet—or Othello, or Lear, or Macbeth—than in knowing what the Shakespearean scholar has to say. From the latter I can learn absolutely nothing—it is all sawdust. But from the nobodies, among whom I include myself, I have everything to learn.

Anyway, it was after I had been out of school some time that, through the tenacity and insatiable curiosity of a Scotch friend of mine—Bill Dyker was his name—my curiosity in Hamlet was awakened. We agreed one night, after a long discussion about Shakespeare and his supposed value to the world, that it would be a good thing to read him again. We also discussed at length that night the question of which play we would tackle first. It's almost inevitable that, when this question comes up, as you've probably noticed, Hamlet shall be *the* play. (This, too, is extremely fascinating to me—this obsessive recurrence of the one play, as though to say, if you *would* know Shakespeare then by all means read Hamlet. Hamlet! Hamlet! Why *Hamlet* always?)

And so we read the play. We had agreed beforehand to get together at a certain date and discuss the play in the light of our individual reactions. Well, the night came, and we met. It so happened, however, that my friend Bill Dyker had also made a date that night to meet a woman uptown. She was an unusual woman, too, it seems, and perhaps there was some excuse for postponing the discussion of *Hamlet*. She was a literary woman who was unable to enjoy ordinary intercourse because "she was built too small." That's how my friend Dyker put it to me, at least. I remember how we started walking uptown in the rain that evening, along Broadway. Somewhere in the Forties we ran across a whore. (It was before the war and the whores were still walking the streets, both by day and night. The saloons were going full blast too.) The strange thing about this meeting was—a coincidence, you will see—that this whore was also a "literary" woman. She had been a writer for the pulps and she had gone under. Before that she had been a dance hall jane in Butte, Montana. Anyway, it was most natural to start in with "literature" and work up. It also happened that that night I had under my arm a book called *Esoteric Buddhism*. (At that time, I was intent upon reading only the "best" books, those that broadened the mind.) It wasn't long, of course, before the whore herself assumed first importance. She was of Irish stock, weak and lovable, and possessed with the usual gift of gab. In addition she was dogmatic. We were dogmatic too. In those days everybody was dogmatic. You could afford to be. When, by a natural process, we finally got to the point the whore of course was disgusted to think that we were going to keep a date with a woman whose predicament was such as I described to you. Furthermore, she didn't believe the story. She said it was incredible. She said, which was the truth, as we discovered later, that the woman was probably a nymphomaniac. It was a delicate situation. *A time to act!* But action was precisely what we were incapable of, even in those days.

The only thing to do, since we couldn't come to a decision was to keep on drinking. We left the saloon we were in and went to a French bar in the Thirties somewhere. They were shooting dice at the bar when we blew in, and my friend Dyker had a passion for dice. There were also a few whores at the bar and, despite the girl at our elbow, they began making overtures to us. The situation kept growing steadily worse, the whore intent on making us and thinking, since we seemed impervious to her physical charms, that it must be her intellect which appealed to us. And so, gradually, we came back to *Hamlet*, very much involved now with the subject of going to bed or not going to bed, the dangers of disease (which went on in asides), the money problem, the question of honor, of keeping our word with the other woman, etc., etc. From this strange bog in which Hamlet became mired I have never been able to extricate him. As for Ophelia, she is inseparable in my mind from a tow-haired girl who was sitting in the back room and whom I had to pass on my way to the toilet every now and then. I remember the pathetic, stupefied look on this girl's face; when later I saw somewhere an illustration of Ophelia floating face up, the hair braided and tangled in the pond lilies, I thought of the girl in the back room of the bar, her eyes glazed, her hair straw-like, as Ophelia's. As for Hamlet himself, my friend Dyker with his "judicial mind" was the quintessence of all the Hamlets I have ever met. He was incapable of making even the decision to empty his bowels. A fact! He used to have a note hanging on the wall of his den reading: "Don't forget to go to the toilet!" His friends, seeing the note, would have to remind him of it. Otherwise he'd have died of constipation. A little later, when he fell in love with a girl and began to think about marrying her, the problem which plagued him was what to do about the sister. The two sisters were practically inseparable. It was like him, of course, to fall in love with both of them. Sometimes the three of them would go to bed together, pretending to take a nap. And while the one sister slept he would make merry with the other. It was quite immaterial to him *which* sister. I remember his painful endeavors to explain all this to me. We used to go over it night after night, seeking a solution . . .

My close friendship with Bill Dyker, you can readily see, got the upper hand of *Hamlet*. Here was a Hamlet in life, one whom I could study at leisure without pain of research. Now that I think of it, how characteristic that from that night when we were going to "discuss" Hamlet the latter died, never to be mentioned by either of us again. Nor do I think that from that day on Bill Dyker ever read another book. Not even *my* book, which I handed him on arriving in New York and of which he said to me, when leaving—"I'll try to get around to reading it sometime, Henry." As though I had imposed a heavy duty on him which, out of longstanding friendship, he would do his best to discharge.

I meant to tell you my impressions of Hamlet as they seeped through during years of wandering, years of idle talk, years of browsing through this and that. How, in the course of time, Hamlet got mixed up with all the other books I have read and forgotten, so that today Hamlet is absolutely amorphous, absolutely polyglot—in a word, universal, like the elements themselves. In the first place, whenever I utter the name there registers immediately an image of Hamlet, an image of a darkened stage on which a pale, thin man with a poetic mop of hair stands in hose and doublet orating to a skull which is held in his extended right hand. (Bear in mind, please, that I have never seen *Hamlet* acted!) In the back of the stage is an open grave about which the earth is heaped up. A lantern reposes on the mound of dirt. Hamlet is talking—talking the utmost gibberish, as far as I can make out. He has been standing there like that, talking, for centuries. The curtain never falls. The speech is never terminated. What should happen after this scene I have always imagined in some such fashion as this, though of course it never really happens. In the midst of the skull talk a courier arrives—probably one of the Guildenstern-Rosenkranz boys. The courier whispers something in Hamlet's ear which Hamlet, being a dreamer, naturally ignores. Suddenly three men in black capes appear and draw their swords. Avaunt! they cry, and with that Hamlet, ridiculously lightening-like and unexpected, draws his sword and the fight's on. The men are killed, of course, in short order. Killed with the lightening-like rapidity of a dream, leaving Hamlet to stare at his bloody sword as a few moments previous he was staring at the skull. Only now—*speechless!*

That's what I see, as I say, when Hamlet's name is mentioned.

Always the same scene, always the same characters, same lantern, same gestures, same words. And always, at the end, *speechless*. That, I think, from my scanty reading of Freud, is decidedly a wish fulfillment. And I am grateful to Freud for learning so.

So far so good—as to images. When I *talk* about Hamlet another mechanism gets into operation. This is what I call the "free fantasia." When this stew gets rattling around in my brain I do my best thinking about Hamlet. Hamlet is in the dead center, with a rapier in his hand. I see the ghost—not of Hamlet, but of Macbeth—stalking the stage. Hamlet addressed it. The ghost vanishes and the play begins. That is, the play *around* Hamlet. Hamlet does nothing—he does not even kill the swift couriers at the end, as I imagine when just the bare name is pronounced. No, Hamlet is standing there in the center of the stage and people are poking and prodding him, as though he were a dead jellyfish cast up on the ocean shore. This goes on for maybe twelve acts, during which time a great many people are killed, or else kill themselves. *All to talk*, understand. The best speeches are always made the moment before death. But none of these speeches advance us anywhere. It's like Lewis Carroll's checkerboard. First you're standing outside a castle and it's raining—an English rain which is good for the swede and turnip crop and for the making of fine woolens. Then there is thunder and lightening, and maybe the ghost reappears. Hamlet talks to the ghost familiarly, easily—because talk is his *metier*. Between times messengers come and go. They whisper now in Hamlet's ear, now in the queen's ear, now in Polonius' ear. A buzz buzz that goes on throughout the whole twelve acts. Polonius comes out now and then in a dunce cap. He has his son Laertes in hand and he brushes the dandruff affectionately from Laertes' coat collar. He does this to throw dust in Hamlet's eye. Hamlet is sullen, and now and then taciturn. He puts his hand on the hilt of his rapier. His eyes flash. Then Ophelia comes out, with her long flaxen hair hanging in braids down her shoulder. She walks with hands clasped over her stomach, mumbling the rosary and looking coy, demure, a little silly withal. She pretends not to notice Hamlet who is standing right in her path. She picks a buttercup by the way and holds it to her nostrils. Hamlet, convinced that she is not all there, makes advances to her—by way of passing the time. This precipitates a drama. It means that Hamlet and his best friend, Laertes, must fight a duel to the death. Hamlet, always loath to act, nevertheless kills his friend Laertes in quick fashion, sighing as he plunges the rapier through his beloved friend's body. Hamlet sighs constantly throughout the play. It's a way of informing the audience that he is not in a cataleptic trance. And after each murder he scrupulously cleans his sword—cleans it with the kerchief that Ophelia dropped on her way out. There is something about Hamlet's gestures which remind one instinctively of the English gentleman. That is why I asked you before if the play occurs in England. For me it's England and nobody can convince me to the contrary. It's the very heart of England, too, I should say somewhere in the neighborhood of Sherwood Forest. The Queen Mother is a virago. She has false teeth, as had all the English queens from time immemorial. She has also a high stomach which in the end invites Hamlet's sword. Somehow I can't detach her from the image of the red Queen in the *Alice* tale. She seems to be talking about butter all the time, how to make it creamy and palatable. Whereas Hamlet is concerned only with Death. The conversation between these two of necessity takes on a strange hue. Surrealistic we would call it today. And yet it's very much to the point. Hamlet suspects his mother of concealing a foul crime. He suspects that he was fouled in the nest. He accuses his mother openly, but she, being given to tergiversation, always manages to turn the conversation back to butter. In fact, in her sly English way, she almost makes Hamlet believe that he himself is guilty of some monstrous crime, just what is never revealed. Hamlet cordially detests his mother. He would strangle her with his bare hands, if he could. But the Queen Mother is too slippery for him. She gets his uncle to put on a play in which Hamlet is made to seem foolish. Hamlet stalks out of the hall before the play is finished. In the vestibule he meets Guildenstern and Rosenkranz. They whisper something in his ear. He says he will go away, on a voyage. They persuade him not to go. He goes out into the garden, by the moat, and in the midst of his reverie he suddenly espies the dead Ophelia floating down the stream, her hair neatly braided, her hands clasped demurely over her stomach. She seems to be smiling in her sleep.

Nobody knows how many days she has been in the water or why the body looks so natural when by all the laws of nature it should now be bloated with gas. Anyway, Hamlet decides to make a speech. He starts in with that famous one—"to be or not to be . . ." Ophelia is floating gently downstream, her ears stopped, but still smiling sweetly as is expected of the English upper classes, even in death. It is this sickly sweet smile of a waterlogged corpse which enrages Hamlet. He doesn't mind Ophelia's death—it's the smile which drives him mad. Again he draws the rapier, and with blood in his eyes, he makes for the banquet hall. Suddenly we are in Denmark, at the castle of Elsinore. Hamlet is a complete stranger, a ghost come to life. He rushes in, intending to murder them all in cold blood. But he is met by his uncle, the erstwhile king. The uncle, full of blandishments, escorts Hamlet to the head of the table. Hamlet refuses to eat. He is fed up with the whole show. He demands to know outright who killed his father, a fact which had completely escaped his attention throughout but of which he is suddenly reminded now that it is time to eat. There is a clatter of dishes and a general hubbub. Polonius, thinking to smooth matters over, tries to make a pretty speech about the weather. Hamlet stabs him behind the arras. The king, feigning not to notice the occurrence, raises the goblet to his lips and bids Hamlet make a toast. Hamlet quaffs the poison goblet, but does not die immediately. Instead the kind himself falls dead at Hamlet's feet. Hamlet runs him through like a piece of cold pork, with his sword. Then, turning to the Queen Mother, he runs her through the stomach—gives her the high enema for once and all. At this moment Guildenstern and Rosenkranz appear. They draw their swords. Hamlet is growing weak. He sinks to a chair. The grave-diggers appear with the lantern and spades. They hand Hamlet a skull. Hamlet takes the skull in his right hand and holding it away from him addresses it in eloquent language. Hamlet is now dying. He knows that he is dying. So he begins his last and best speech which, unfortunately, is never terminated. Rosenkranz and Guildenstern sneak out by the back door. Hamlet is left alone at the banquet table, the floor strewn with corpses. He is talking a blue streak. The curtain slowly falls . . .

3

November 19, 1935

It may interest you to know that yesterday, according to the newspaper, the Comtesse de Chambrun (the former Clara Long-worth) "departed from her special field of Shakespeare and presented a detailed and *thoughtful* survey of the American novel." Among other things the Comtesse had this to say: "I have already said and would like to repeat that the only quality which differentiates our American production from that of the Old World lies in the superior gift of creative imagination and a humorous vigor born of the soil. But what is earthborn is not necessarily earthy. This is the great mistake of the ultramodernistic school which today holds the center of our stage." "Among the best modern writers," says the Comtesse, "there is always an essential element lacking and I believe Mark Twain has put his finger on it. *America is so given to comedy. We need a tragic tone now and then.*"

And so, in case *Hamlet, our* Hamlet, is not enough, I want you to go to the butcher's today and order two lbs. of tragedy—the best cut, tender, juicy, palatable. Perhaps it was owing to the Comtesse's thoughtful survey of the modern novel that the next day, as if inspired by her words, a cyclist pedaling up a hill on the outskirts of Geneva "suddenly exploded and fell dead with smoke coming out of his head." Seems he had been carrying a dynamite cartridge in his mouth and suddenly it occurred to him to bite and he bit. It's possible, of course, that the Comtesse may not consider this proper material for tragedy. This is just a newspaper item and there are no covers around it. It couldn't be acted day in and day out, a thing like this. So far there have been no tragedies in which a man suddenly exploded and fell dead with smoke coming out of his head. These are not Shakespearean tragedies—just newspaper tragedies.

And now, with these few prefatory remarks, I want to answer the question you pose with regard to my preface to *Bastard Death*. You know, of course, that in asking me to "explain" these pages you are asking me to violate myself.

For myself the clue to these first three pages, begun in jest as an addenda to *Black Spring*, to be entitled "I the Human Being," lies in the sentence: "It means, to use the language of the day, that the Ego alone with its Id must create a time space feeling equivalent to the instability of loneliness." This terminology, borrowed from psycho-analysis, raised to nonsense, and counterpointed against a fundamental truth, resurrects the now missing God problem. There are two kinds of loneliness today: the loneliness of the herd which feels that it is being driven over the precipice and the loneliness of the creative individual, now more acute than ever since there is no recoil in the collectivity. The modern neurosis, clearly revealed in the work of the modern artist, expresses itself through *fear of life*. Fear is a constant in the human equation—there is no dispossessing it. But the old irrational phenomena of fear, linked up with the magic of primitive man, gave way, through the building up of Cultures, to a tangible talkable *fear of death*. The creative process, however, stands beyond, outside both the fear of death and the fear of life. (For the fear of life, which we have today, is but the admission of the breakdown of the cultural form.) The question which concerns us vitally is not the death of art, but the drying up of the creative faculty.

In positing the idea of *The Sacred Body* you imply a loneliness which has no equivalent in the modern man. This loneliness was brought about by the peculiar sort of Absolute inherent in our Culture. This Absolute was the monotheistic God of the Jews. Frozen and remote, the Jewish Jehovah became the sole source of terror. By means of this relationship man was able to shoulder a burden of guilt never before known. The legend of Christ owes its power to the deep wish of man to transfer this load—to get out from under, as it were. By believing in Him, Christ, by faith alone were we supposed to be absolved from all sin. The example He gave us was a brilliant one, but in raising himself to a symbol he worked a fiasco on us, or rather his hagiographers did.

And now before continuing this further I want to make a grand detour—as a result of our long drawn-out discussion last night. I want you to bear in mind, however, as we momentarily forsake the precise theme of this letter, that the objective I have in mind is an *impossible* one. Far more important to me than the clarification of these pages (1 to 3 of the Preface) which, by the way, we ought to include in this book as an Appendix, is the clarification of a natural difference in our attitude towards things. It was inevitable that last night, starting with the problem of purpose and method of art, that we should end on the discord of integrity and honesty. For a long time I have kept among my files certain quotations from other writers which have a tremendous significance for me, more particularly because the expression of these various ideas seems to me so exact—not "true" or "false," I would have you understand, but "exact."

And since the very nexus of our whole discussion was the question of an attitude towards Ideas I am going to quote for you first of all one which goes to the very heart of the subject . . .

"The problem which X set out to solve was this: how comes it about that with consciously false ideas we yet reach conclusions that are in harmony with Nature and appeal to us as Truth? That we do so is obvious, especially in the 'exact' branches of science. In mathematics it is notorious that we start from absurdities to reach a realm of law, and our whole conception of the nature of the world is based on a foundation which we believe to have no existence . . . Fiction is, indeed, an indispensable supplement to logic, or even a part of it; whether we are working inductively or deductively, both ways hang closely together with fiction; and axioms, though they seek to be primary verities, are more akin to fiction . . . the representative world is a system of fictions. It is a symbol by the help of which we orient ourselves. The business of science is to make the symbol ever more adequate, but it remains a symbol, a means of action, for action is the last end of thinking . . .

"X is throughout careful to distinguish fiction alike from hypothesis and dogma ... The fiction is impossible but it enables us to reach what for us is relatively truth ... God, the Soul, Immortality, the Moral World-Order: the critical hearers understand what is meant when these great words are used, and if the uncritical misunderstood, that, adds X, may sometimes be also useful. For these things are Ideals, and all Ideals are, logically speaking, fictions. As science leads to the Imaginary, so Life leads to the Impossible; without them we cannot reach to the heights we are born to scale. Taken literally, however, our most valuable conceptions are worthless.

"We can only regard reality as a Heraclitean flux of happening—and our thinking would itself be fluid if it were not that by fiction we obtain imaginary stand-points and boundaries by which to gain control of the flow of reality. *It is the special art and object of thinking to attain existence itself. But the wish by so doing to understand the world is both unrealizable and foolish, for we are only trying to comprehend our own fictions. We can never solve the so-called world riddle* because what seems riddles to us are merely the contradictions we have ourselves created. Yet though the way of thinking cannot be the way of being, since they stand on such different foundations, thinking always has a kind of parallelism with being, and though we make our reckoning with a reality that we falsify, yet the practical results tend to come out right ... We may make distinctions between practical scientific thinking and disinterested aesthetic thinking. *Yet all thinking is finally a comparison.* Scientific fictions are parallel with aesthetic fictions. The poet is the type of all thinkers: there is no sharp boundary between the region of poetry and the region of science. Both alike are not ends in themselves, but means to higher ends ... All thinking is a regulated error ... It is in choice and regulation of our errors, in our readiness to accept ever-closer approximations to the unattainable reality, that we think rightly and live rightly ... A man is what he loves!" I am coming eventually to the Chinese conception of art and life with which I am in complete sympathy and which, I believe, for the moment marks the quality of difference in our approach to life. Before doing so I quote once again ...

"However we look at it, we see that Man, whether he works individually or collectively, may conveniently be regarded, in the comprehensive sense, as an artist, a bad artist, maybe, for the most part, but still an artist. His civilization—if that is the term we choose to apply to the sum total of his group activities—is always an art, or a complex of arts. It is an art that is to be measured or left immeasurable. That question, we have seen, we may best leave open. Another question that might be put is easy to deal with more summarily: What is Art? We may deal with it summarily because it is an ultimate question and there can be no final answer to such ultimate questions. As soon as we begin to ask such questions, as soon as we begin to look at any phenomenon as an end in itself, we are on the perilous slope of metaphysics, where no agreement can, or should be, possible. It is no accident that poetry, which has so often seemed the typical art, means a *making*. The artist is a maker ... For a cat is an artist as well as a man, and some would say more than a man while a bee is not only an obvious artist, but perhaps even the typical natural and unconscious artist. There is no defining art; there is only the attempt to distinguish between good art and bad art ... Yet creation, in the active visible constructive sense, is not the whole of Man. It is not even the whole of what Man has been accustomed to call God. When, by what is now termed a process of Narcissism, Man created God in his own image, as may be instructively observed in the first chapter of the Hebrew book of Genesis, he assigned to him six parts of active creational work, and one part of passive contemplation of that work. That one seventh part—and an immensely important part—has not come under our consideration. In other words, we have been looking at Man the artist, not at Man the aesthetician. To confuse art and aesthetics leads to a lamentable confusion. The distinction between the two is never sufficiently emphasized—i.e., distinction between the dynamic and the static aspects of human action. Herein is the whole difference between work, for art is essentially work, and the spectacular contemplation of work, which aesthetics essentially is. The two things are ultimately one ... but they must be kept apart ...

"That was the elaborately developed argument of Schopenhauer: art ... is useless. 'To be useless is the mark of genius, its patent of nobility.' All other works of men are there for the preservation or alleviation of our existence; but this alone is there for its own sake;

and is in this sense to be regarded as the flower, or the pure essence, of existence . . . 'Genius,' said Z, 'is the most complete objectivity.' Most of us, it seems to Z, never see reality at all; we only see the labels we have fixed on things to mark for us their usefulness. A veil is interposed between us and the reality of things. The artist, the man of genius, raises this veil and reveals Nature to us. He is naturally endowed with a detachment from life, and so possesses as it were a virginal freshness in seeing, hearing, or thinking. That is 'intuition,' an instinct that has become disinterested. 'Art,' says Z, 'has no other object but to remove the practically useful symbols, the conventional and socially accepted generalities, so as to bring us face to face with reality itself . . .'

"It is through Plotinus that we realize how aesthetics is on the same plane, if not one, with mysticism. For by his insistence on Contemplation, which is Aesthetics, we learn to understand what is meant when it is said, as it often is, that mysticism is Contemplation. The artist for art's sake—and the same is constantly found true of the scientist for science's sake—in turning aside from the common utilitarian aims of men is really engaged in a task none other can perform, of immense utility to men. The Cistercians of old hid their cloisters in forests and wilderness far from society, mixing not with men nor performing for them so-called useful tasks; yet they spent their days and nights in chant and prayer, working for the salvation of the world, and they stand as symbol of all higher types of artists, not the less so because they, too, illustrate that faith transcending sight, without which no art is possible . . . Every great artist, a Dante or a Shakespeare, a Dostoievski or a Proust, thus furnishes the metaphysical justification of existence by the beauty of the vision he presents of the cruelty and the horror of existence. All the pain and the madness, even the ugliness and the commonplace of the world, he converts into shining jewels. By revealing the spectacular character of reality he restores the serenity of its innocence.

"So it is that in art lies the solution of the conflicts of philosophy. There we see Realism, or the discovery of things, one with Idealism, or the creation of things. Art is the embodied harmony of their conflict. That could not be more exquisitely symbolized than by these two supreme figures in the spiritual life of Europe—the Platonic

Socrates and the Gospel Jesus, both alike presented to us, it is so significant to observe, as masters of irony."

And now for China.

"The quality of play in the Chinese character and civilization has impressed alike those who have seen China from afar and by actual contact . . . All toys are popular . . . They have an elaborate form of chess, far more difficult than ours . . . Y remarks how this simple childlike, yet profound attitude towards life results in a liberation of the impulses to play and enjoyment which 'makes Chinese life unbelievably restful and delightful after the solemn cruelties of the West . . .' Life is regulated by ceremony and music . . . It is on the earth and not in the skies that the Confucian Heaven lies concealed . . . The sphere in which ceremonies act is Man's external life; his internal life is the sphere of music. It is music that molds the manners and customs that are comprised under ceremony . . . It is music that regulates the heart and mind and with that development brings joy, and joy brings repose. And so 'Man became Heaven.' 'Let ceremonies and music have their course until the earth is filled with them.! . . .'

"We may understand now how it is that in China, and in China alone among the great surviving civilizations, we find that art animates the whole of life, even its morality. 'This universal presence of art, manifested in the smallest utensil, the humblest stalls, the notices on the shops, the handwriting, the rhythm of movement, always regular and measured, as though to the time of unheard music, announces a civilization which is complete in itself, elaborated in the smallest detail, penetrated by one spirit, which no interruption ever breaks, a harmony which becomes at length a hallucinatory and overwhelming obsession.' 'For them the art of life is one, as this world and the other are one. Their aim is to make the Kingdom of Heaven here and now.' It is obvious that a natural temperament in which the art-impulse is so all-embracing, and the aesthetic sensibility so acute, might well have been of a perilous instability. We could scarcely have been surprised if, like that surpassing episode in Egyptian history of which Akhenaton was the leader and Tel-el-Amarna the tomb, it had only endured for a moment. Yet Chinese civilization, which has throughout shown the dominating power of this sensitive temperament, has lasted longer than any other. The reason is that the very excesses of their temperament forced the Chinese to fortify themselves against its perils. The Great Wall, built more than 2,000 years ago, and still today almost the most impressive work of man on earth, is typical of this attitude of the Chinese. They have exercised a stupendous energy in fortifying themselves against the natural enemies of their own temperament... Alike in its large outlines and its small details, Chinese life is always the art of balancing an aesthetic temperament and guarding against its excesses... Thus, during its extremely long history... Chinese civilization has borne witness to the great fact that all human life is art. It may be because they have realized this so thoroughly that the Chinese have been able to preserve their civilization so long, through all the violent shocks to which it has been subjected." This leads me back to my habitual, stubborn, illogical defense of the French whom Spengler so willfully misunderstands. For to my mind the French (and not the Germans, as Nietzsche so unjustly said) are the Chinese of Europe. What Nietzsche intended as an insult to the Germans I consider a tribute to the French. And though I myself have nothing in common with the French, though I regard myself as absolutely alien to them, from head to toe, being myself in the damnable Hamlet-Faust tradition, I respect them and admire them. For when the day comes on which this European civilization falls apart—when Paris, Berlin, Rome, London, New York fall—it will be the Mediterranean spirit which will survive in the new Culture—altered and disguised, of course— and not the Faustian spirit. I say this dogmatically because there is in the Mediterranean attitude towards life that art germ which has been strangled and well-nigh obliterated by the morose, northern mind. And if, to use your own logic, we take the Jewish spirit as index of the trend, then notice please that in France the Jew is almost wiped out as Jew, that is, absorbed, assimilated, Mediterraneanized. Her great artists, inventors, thinkers, men of affairs, present themselves to our mind, particularly when Jewish, as eminently French. In each individual Frenchman there lingers the traces of a Culture which, owing to the creative genius of an alien spirit, has been mistakenly identified with "Western" culture. France occupies a spiritual latitude which connects the vital past with the vital future. Her two-thousand year old kiss may be abhorrent and repulsive to you, but it is still a kiss and not an act of cannibalism. That very eye with which you see owes the greater part of its visionary faculty to a spirit which is alien to your own blood. If you want to kiss with new lips then you must also learn to see with new eyes.

And when you have grown new lips and new eyes we will recommence the Cancer concerts a la Hamlet. For this is *our* Hamlet, this restless striving towards a fixed doubt of which we are incapable.

4

November 20, 1935

Your book, *Bastard Death*, reopening for me the subject of Schizophrenia, it's metaphysical and artistic significance. Reopened, I might also say, the whole subject of the Hamlet-Faust mechanism about which I had intended to write so much. Just as Proust's great work symbolized for me the ultimate elaboration of the Hamlet theme, so your work appeared to present the ultimate elaboration of the Faustian counterpart. In the Titanic rage and disorder of Shakespeare's work I long visualized to myself the germination of that tempest in a teapot which was later to manifest itself, through the phenomenon of Schizophrenia, as the polar tension between the two Absolutes created by the spiritual drama in our entrails.

Surely Hamlet was not the first schizoid type to appear in the world. But the sway and preponderance of Hamlet is significant. Just as Dante symbolizes the whole spirit of the Middle Ages, its cosmogonic unity, so Hamlet symbolizes the spirit of the modern age. The scholar would no doubt have preferred Da Vinci to Hamlet, but in my opinion Da Vinci is an anomaly, a symbol of the possible rather than the actual. Thinking of Hamlet then in his symbolic aspect I regard it as a fact of prime importance that the speech most generally associated with his name is the one beginning "To be or not to be . . ." If this were all that remained today of Shakespeare's play we might, like Cuvier, reconstruct the whole skeleton of the drama.

When Spengler, in a characteristic piece of Faustian logic, tries to separate Leonardo from the other great artists of his period by emphasizing the fact that he was "essentially the artist of torsos" he means to say, as I understand it, that this searching, roaming spirit, *this discoverer*, symbolized his own plight by giving us the image of the truncated body. For in a footnote which reveals the Faustian bias, he adds: "In Renaissance work the finished product is often quite depressingly complete. The absence of "infinity" is palpable. No secrets, no discoveries." "His soul," he says, "was lost afar in the future, though his mortal part, his eye and hand, obeyed the spirit of the age." He talks of Leonardo investigating the *life* in the body, and not the body itself. The *investigation* of life! How modern that sounds! How horrible!

How Spengler loves to dwell on this enigmatic figure of Leonardo! A *discoverer through and through*, he says. "The first man to set his mind to work on aviation. To fly, to free one's self from earth, to lose one's self in the expanse of the universe—is not this ambition Faustian in the highest degree?" Leonardo *is* already over the frontier, he concludes. Yes, poor Leonardo! Half of him stuck in the sands, the other half winging on through space—still *investigating* life probably. What is it we feel about Leonardo's mysterious figures, I ask you? What mystery is it that lurks in these seraphic, beautific countenances? Is it the conquest of space by the aeroplane, is it the Big Bertha, is it the electro-dynamic plate? Or is it the absence of *balls*? Or do these things go together? For me, when I look at one of Leonardo's portraits, there comes a feeling of revulsion, of abysmal disgust, of loathing. I see no mystery in these faces. I see a bearded old man in skirts, a man without God who oscillates in his creations between the throes of cannibalism and the throes of castration.

I want to tell you a little more about Leonardo and his famous "Lord's Supper" which I remember studying from earliest childhood. (The Lord's Supper! Did you ever stop to think what a mealy piece of spiritual claptrap lies in that phrase? Supper for the Lord! How Jewish! How Kosher!) Anyway, speaking of the reproduction which used to hang on the wall in Glendale, where I used to pass my first vacations, how well I remember the stifling effect of this great work on me when I used to enter the little bedroom where I slept with Joey and Tony. They were my little pals from the country, Joey and

Tony, and they were being raised in the Catholic faith. The room was full of holy images, rosaries, crucifixes, bleeding hearts, etc., etc. It was like entering a morgue, the private morgue of our Lord Jesus Christ. At the foot of the bed was this fucking "Lord's supper" which I'm telling you about. It was an engraving, I suppose, absolutely devoid of color, absolutely devoid of life. There was a huge table, such as you now write on, but no food on the table. There were goblets for wine, but I couldn't see any wine flowing. It was very sad, very dismal. The Lord was being betrayed, or had already been betrayed, I don't remember clearly. As I say, there was no food on the table that I can recall. Either they had already eaten, or they were about to eat, though from the expressions on their faces food seemed to be about the last thing on their minds. It was a spiritual banquet in which our Lord was going to pour out his own blood and make them drunk forever. Later, when I came to Plato's *"Banquet,"* I realized that there are two kinds of feasts in this world, the one in which, as Herman Melville says, the body is nourished with champagne and oysters and the other in which the soul is nourished with imaginary wine, "sacrificial wine" it's called. Even as a kid I had the feeling that these soulish banquets were dead affairs and not for me. I never observed, for example, any imaginary feasting in the houses where the "Lord's Supper" was hung up. Nobody ever stood up, in these homes, and suddenly announced that he would give a pint of blood to wipe out our sins. No siree! All these good Catholics drank real wine, or generally beer and whiskey, sometimes a bit of *schnapps.* When they sat down to table they demanded good joints of mutton, chopped spinach with egg, potato dumplings, black gravy, cornstarch pudding, figs, nuts, cheese, and so forth. I never asked anybody, when I was a kid, what was the meaning of this picture on the wall. A picture was a picture to me, and I took it for what it was worth. What interested me more than anything then was the costumes which the disciples were wearing. I used to be perplexed about their sex, because they had beards and they wore skirts. I felt that perhaps this was peculiar only to holy men and as I had never met a holy man I was content to let it rest as an enigma. When I grew up and read about great painting I was amazed to discover that one of the great qualities about this fresco was its architectonics. All along I had gotten to believe that the first virtue of this picture was its religious quality. I must say that to this day I remain baffled by it. I see nothing but this bleak, dismal table without food, a bunch of togaed Jews, and a very pale, frail, feminine, spiritual looking man, Our Lord, who seems to be the master of ceremonies. Where the feast takes place I haven't the slightest idea. It might be a stable, for all I know. I know it's dark and gloomy, and every time I think of it I get the feeling of bat-wings brushing my lips. And what I say to myself now is this—if this was intended to be the representation of a sublime moment in our spiritual life then it's a fiasco, because I don't get the slightest feeling of sublimity from it. If, on the other hand, it was intended to be a masterpiece of draftsmanship, then I say I'd rather any day go and look at the Brooklyn Bridge." If the "mortal part" of him made this picture then the immortal part was certainly missing. The hand and eye may have been there, but where were the *balls?* I have attended spiritual banquets and enjoyed them, but they were never *fake* banquets. The Egyptians, when they celebrated the "Feast of the Dead," ate real food, drank real wine, had real talk. Even the corpse which they paraded was real. It was not an *imaginary* corpse. They were so real, these dead bodies, that some of them, I do believe, will outlast our pale Saviour whose imaginary blood was to wipe out our imaginary sins.

5

November 23, 1935

By a remarkable coincidence I passed from my little disquisition on "The Last Supper" to Aldous Huxley's "Meditation on El Greco," more particularly a meditation on El Greco's "Dream of Philip II." And from that, by a still more striking coincidence, to another little essay of Huxley's, in the same volume, entitled "The Rest is Silence." And between these I rediscovered my old friend, Pierre Mille, whose passage on the *Pavillion des Femmes* I chopped out of the *Tropic of Cancer* to my everlasting regret.

And now here is how Aldous Huxley opens his little essay called "The Rest Is Silence . . ."

"From pure sensation to the intuition of beauty, from pleasure and pain to love and the mystical ecstasy and death—all the things that are fundamental, all the things that, to the human spirit, are most profoundly significant, can only be experienced, not expressed. The rest is always and everywhere silence . . . Music's ability to express the inexpressible was recognized by the greatest of all verbal artists. The man who wrote *Othello* and *The Winter's Tale* was capable of uttering in words whatever words can possibly be made to signify. And yet (I am here indebted to a very interesting essay by Mr. Wilson Knight), and yet whenever something in the nature of a mystical emotion or intuition had to be communicated, Shakespeare regularly called upon music to help him to 'put it across.' "

It seems to me, from the foregoing, that Mr. Huxley is not only slightly muddled, but that he contradicts himself. To say that

Shakespeare was capable of uttering in words whatever words can possible be made to signify is to credit him with a potential omnipotence which is ridiculous and idolatrous. It also creates one of those false barriers between the art of music and the art of literature which explains nothing. In making Shakespeare the God of words Mr. Huxley very conveniently posits another realm which is meant to exonerate his God from the charge of not being omnipotent. There were other writers, and greater writers than Shakespeare who, in my opinion proved capable of expressing in words those things of a mystical or intuitive nature for which Shakespeare had to invoke the aid of music. It is strange that, in going over the manuscript of my last book, I excised as being irrelevant and unimportant a passage on music in which I made direct reference to Mr. Huxley. I think the moment is opportune to introduce it here . . .

"We have a slipshod way of saying that 'music' expresses the inexpressible.' Music expresses music. Isn't that sufficient? In the music of Beethoven there is an approximation of the highest order to what most of us talk about a great deal and none of us know anything about—God. One has the feeling, in listening to Beethoven, of approaching the ultimate. The ultimate of what? of music? Of something, certainly. This ultimate something which Mr. Huxley's Stavrogin, Spandrell, detects an A Minor Quartet annihilates him. It is not the bullet that kills Spandrell—Mr. Huxley is at great pains to make that clear. It is the God in the wax record that does the trick. Chamber music is the great lethal invention of the Occident. It is pure suicide. And of all the forms of annihilation which we covert a Beethoven quartet is perhaps the most sublime. It is *pure* annihilation as distinguished from lesser, muddier annihilations. There is nothing to be mopped up afterwards. Perfection and consistency. Dire consistency. Finish. Permanence. It makes one despair. It permeates everything one does and kills the desire to do, even *to be*. Sometimes, when a little phrase bursts forth, swells suddenly out of nothingness like a sail taking the wind, like a wing spreading, one has the feeling that it is impossible ever to exhaust the content and significance of this little phrase. You want to hang on to it in the utter bliss of non-being. Not Gothic alone, not

Christian, nor even pagan thought can sum up what lies behind this little phrase. A whole universe of thought and feeling is contained in it, and said to say, it is a universe of which we have not the slightest knowledge. Even when one recognizes the "influence," even when one hears Mozart and the whole 18th century of form, grace, reason, elegance, dignity, etc., in this phrase, still one hears beyond these—one hears the whole cycle of life which led up to this culminating point called Beethoven. One feels Beethoven rushing us up to the edge of the precipice and flinging himself over—*and us with him!* While Goethe, calm, serene, Olympian, mantled in the full shroud of two centuries straddles the fence. Goethe remains behind like the leaning tower of Pisa, fixed in the perpetual act of falling. But with Beethoven it is like a wheel of light forming a jewel and some Satanic impulse casting the jewel down into the bottomless pit. Beethoven seems to eject whole men, whole epochs, whole continents, out of his light-form. One feels the hardness, the grit, the unquenchable corolla of light, and with a despairing exultation, one feels at the same time the mad, the insane, the ordained impulse which bade him throw himself over the brink. There are times when, at the fullest measure of control, like a seer weaving his spell, Beethoven, in order to make the ultimate manifest, suddenly rises upon the firmament of the imagination like a Titan and, with one, fierce, abrupt, demonic blow, smashes it all to smithereens. Saying "I, Beethoven, I created it! I, Beethoven, I destroy it!"

And so, when in your postscript dated the 22nd you ask—"are music and poetry anti-thought processes? Is the counter-drive to thought the more powerful drive? Is perhaps life itself a counter-drive to thought?"—I answer *Yes, Yes, Yes.* The answer Yes is based on a temporary agreement as to the supposition created by your very questions. For here you make thought the dead thing which it is not *per se*; here you make thought and poetry antithetical, which they are not *per se*; here you put thought and life in opposition, which is not so *per se*. But I follow you. Your mistake lies in making thought an end in itself.

You speak a great deal about clarity and order in your letter, about the need for heroism—and about labor pains. I hope you don't mean to imply by this last that the labor pains are more important than the product itself? Heroism is something I have always associated with deeds. Kant is no hero to me, nor Schopenhauer either. Nietzche yes, because he put up a valiant fight to have his brainchild recognized. It was his fight with the world which makes him an interesting figure to me. It was not a fight against windmills, *a la Don Quixote*. That Kant had huge lungs and a huge stomach might, as you seem to imply, make him a great philosopher, but it does not make a *man*. And if his labor pains were great the product of his labor remains nevertheless dull, uninteresting, unimportant *to me*. Kant was the personification of a system of thought, even down to his daily walk. Perhaps if he called on God to help him the results of his labors might be more entertaining, if not more edifying. I can live without Kant and his metaphysical gas bag. In *his* case I should say, answering another of your questions, that "thought is a disease."

Much of what you say about Hamlet is incomprehensible to me. In some peculiar way you've identified him with heroism. That strikes me as very strange because I've always regarded him as the very symbol of cowardice. Perhaps cowardice is too strong a word. *Frustration*, to use the modern parlance, would be better. He was incapable of action, that is the point. Thought becomes, with Hamlet, a free wheel, and we are left spinning with him in the void. About Kant at least we can say that he erected his thought into a system, and though that system may be utterly repugnant, utterly useless to most of us, nevertheless it bears the stamp of creativity. From any standpoint Hamlet is non-creative. You seem to confuse Shakespeare with Hamlet, if I follow your logic. As Hamlet Shakespeare was creative, but the significance of his creation is to reveal the tragedy of man's non-creative aspect. The reason Hamlet is bogged and sunk finally is because he doubts. It's not that he forsakes action for thought, but because he did not know how to think. He was not a great thinker, Hamlet. In fact, he was no thinker at all. He was a late Sophist caught in a world of action. Almost at the same time that Hamlet was born there was born another man, a Frenchman, who so successfully identified thinking with life that he remains the single outstanding figure in French culture. He left no philosophy behind him, but he deepened our conception of what it is to be human. Today we have another Frenchman, equally celebrated as a thinker, but the impression he creates in us is that of a thoroughly non-human individual. This is the man who pretends to inform us about the creative process in Leonardo Da Vinci. His essay is absolutely unintelligible to me. I trust you will be able to guess who the two figures are I have in mind. One of them is *not* Rabelais, as you might be inclined to think.

In view of the foregoing I hope it is clear that I do not think "life is a disease." I think that disease is a very great factor in life, but I refuse to identify thought or life as disease. Hamlet is a disease— a disease of the mind. And Hamlet is *not* good for me! Nor do I see any necessity for extending the road back into the past, as you say. For me the road is forward, no matter where it leads. For me the purpose of these pages is to reveal the lingering effects of Hamletism and thus to scotch it. And so I return, by devious routes, to the thought which animated the opening of this letter—to the fact that Aldous Huxley, in an essay on El Greco, revealed a side of himself hitherto unknown and thereby reached to the peak of his being. And, just as with the famous "three pages," though you may not suspect it, there is a relation between this essay on El Greco and all that we have been discussing. For Aldous Huxley this experience of which he writes must have been in the nature of a conversion, just as when sitting in a little cafe on the Boulevard St.-Germain reading that newspaper article by Pierre Mille I too went through a conversion. For it was that morning, at breakfast, that I first entered into the spirit of the French language and consequently into the spirit of French life. On that morning, which I mark as an event in my life, a new language was born to me and by it all things were to be reinterpreted. It was not exactly clear to me what Pierre Mille was talking about—*that* I want you to realize, because that is important in relation to what follows. There was something beyond clarity here—*it was magic*. Today, reading that article again, I would probably find it quite ordinary. But then it was *extraordinary*. And the reason for its extraordinary, its magic hold over me, was because I was just ignorant enough to be susceptible to that which is lost in the fine meshes of order and clarity. I was ripe for an experience and Pierre Mille's article was just suitably couched to permit this experience to be lived. Another writer, one let us say, more capable than Pierre Mille, would have destroyed the possibility of such an experience.

Thus, Aldous Huxley, speaking of this picture of El Greco's—"Dream of Philip II"—writes: "In spite of its mediocrity, it is a picture for which I have a special weakness. I like it for the now sadly unorthodox reason that the subject interests me. And the subject interests me because I do not know what the subject is . . . I do not know—do not at present even desire to know." And then we have, from the pen of one of England's most intelligent writers, one of her most *lucid* writers, a confession of bewilderment, a description of non-comprehension, which makes all other writing about El Greco seem like so much nonsense.

"Solid and three-dimensional," he says, "made to be the inhabitants of a spacious universe, El Greco's people are shut up in a world where there is perhaps just room enough to swing a cat, but no more. They are in prison and, which makes it worse, in a visceral prison. For all that surrounds them is organic, animal. Clouds, rocks, drapery have all been mysteriously transformed into mucus and skinned muscle and peritoneum. The Heaven into which Count Orgaz ascends is like some cosmic operation for appendicitis. The Madrid *Resurrection* is a resurrection in a digestive tube. And from the later pictures we receive the gruesome impression that all the personages, both human and divine, have begun to suffer a process of digestion, are being gradually assimilated to their visceral surroundings . . . Twenty years more, and the Trinity, the Communion of Saints and all the human race would have found themselves reduced to hardly distinguishable excrescences on the surface of a cosmic gut. The most favoured might perhaps have aspired to be taenias and trematodes . . .

"For El Greco belongs as a metaphysician (every significant artist is a metaphysician, a propounder of beauty-truths and form-theories) to no known school. The most one can say, by way of classification, is that, like most of the great artists of the Baroque, he believed in the validity of ecstasy, of the non-rational, 'numinous' experiences out of which, as a raw material, the reason fashions the gods or the various attributes of God . . .

"El Greco seems to be talking all the time about the physiological root of ecstasy, not the spiritual flower; about the primary corporeal facts of numinous experience, not the mental derivatives from them ...

"So far as he is concerned there is nothing outside the whale. The primary physiological fact of religious experience is also, for him, the final fact. He remains consistently on the plane of that visceral consciousness which we so largely ignore, but with which our ancestors (as their language proves) did so much of their feeling and thinking ...

"Teresa knew God in terms of an exquisite pain in her heart, her side, her bowels. But while Teresa, and along with her the generality of human beings, found it natural to pass from the realm of physiology into that of the spirit—from the belly of the whale out into the wide open sky—El Greco obstinately insisted on remaining swallowed. His meditations were all of religious experience and ecstasy—but always of religious experience in its raw physiological state, always of primary, immediate, visceral ecstasy ... For the Christian symbols remind us of all the spiritual open spaces—the open spaces of altruistic feeling, the open spaces of abstract thought, the open spaces of free-floating spiritual ecstasy. El Greco imprisons them, claps them up in a fish's gut. The symbols of the spiritual open spaces are compelled by him to serve as a language in terms of which he talks about the close immediacies of visceral awareness, about the ecstasy that annihilates the personal soul, not by dissolving it out into universal infinity, but by drawing it down and drowning it in the warm, pulsating, tremulous darkness of the body."

Mr. Huxley began this essay with the statement—"the pleasures of ignorance are as great, in their way, as the pleasures of knowledge." He ends on the same note ... "One of these days I may discover what the picture is about, and when that has happened I shall no longer be at liberty to impose my own interpretations. Imaginative criticism is essentially an art of ignorance."

What Mr. Huxley is trying to make clear—has he not unconsciously been making it clear all along?—is that there are two kinds of knowledge, one that kills, and one that gives life. For this "imaginative criticism" which he describes as "essentially an art of ignorance" is undoubtedly another kind of knowledge and, to my way of thinking, an infinitely better sort. This is a knowledge which communicates itself directly. Like the very method which Mr. Huxley attributes to El Greco it is based on a "visceral conscious-ness." Now Mr. Huxley, I feel quite safe in saying would never have written this way about El Greco had he not come in contact with D.H. Lawrence. Though professing, in his Introduction to the "Letters of D.H. Lawrence," to deplore Lawrence's inability to grasp certain scientific truths (Lawrence saying all the time: "but I don't feel it *here*! I don't feel it *here!*") we now see Mr. Huxley catching it in the guts himself, his upper parts being loped off temporarily. And the interesting thing is that, for the moment cured of his encyclopaedic mania, Mr. Huxley manages to convey to us a quality heretofore unnoticed in his work. He is instructive without being pedantic. He does grasp a large truth—through letting his fancy wander, as he says. What amazes me is that, having once grasped his truth, he can backslide again. Undoubtedly he is himself still unaware of the value of his discovery. Or, realizing it, he is unable to avail himself of this truth.

I don't want you to think from all this that Mr. Huxley is an important writer to me. But he has this importance for me—that he represents the plight of so many modern artists who unable to liberate their creative powers fall back on their intellectual faculties. The affinity between Lawrence and Huxley would be inexplicable if it were not so patent that Huxley had a deep need for this visceral consciousness of which he speaks. In Lawrence he recognized a man who, like El Greco, saw nothing outside the body of the whale.

The modern man has a self-patronizing, complacent way of looking upon himself which is particularly nauseating to me. He seems to think that he is infinitely richer in experience than his ancestors simply because the means of communication have been extended. It seems to me that it is precisely the number and variety of possibilities lying open before us which impoverishes us. In the restricted life, aware of its full possibilities—not imagined ones!— I sense the greatest measure of enrichment. All those experiences which refuse to be assimilated by the individual soul—and there are very definite limits to our capacity for experience—create a sense of frustration. The possible hangs over the horizon in a deepening gloom: it paralyzes the will. And all these incomplete experiences are gathered up into a huge brake which clamps down on the wheel of life whenever it threatens to revolve. In all our action there is a tremendous negative tautness, an almost *geologic* fatalism. Which may be producing, way below the crust, the most wonderful veined marble, the most brilliant gems. But it is going on in the dark. Soliloquies on the floor of the ocean.

By a sort of dream premonition the most forward spirits have dropped to the bottom, the very hub, you might say. When they had scraped enough of the crust away to perceive the horror of the void they drowned themselves. They went down with huge stones in their bellies. For such as us these men are lost—lost forever. The men of the coming age, the men who survive the cataclysm, may rediscover them. If they are naive, fearless, innocent—if they are interested in torsos rather than skeletons, in veins rather than in patina.

We talk about the past and future like stageshifters talk about the scenes that are being shuffled back and forth. History is a meaningless decor for the show we never put on. Nothing lives in us, neither in retrospect, nor in anticipation. The present is a vacuum, a painful, frozen state, a sort of gloomy vestibule in which we lie suspended, ready to explode with the least barometric change. In a way we are like those wonderfully preserved objects which are found in the Egyptian tombs; we crumble away upon exposure. We crumble to utter, traceless dust. *Immune!* That is our watchword. No contagion. No disease. A static, sanitary eternity of the present, with ourselves as the culmination of all that has gone before. A sanitary republic of ineffective bacteria! That's us today. With this reality I have no concern. It doesn't exist for me, or rather, it exists intermittently, like a nightmare. It is what I see when I rub my eyes. It is false. It is cardboard. There is another reality, of which the vivid dream is composed, and this reality is the very plasma of life. Rimbaud recognized it, and Proust and Dostoievski, and Lawrence. Van Gogh knew it too. Every tree, every hand, every stone or chair or flower he painted testified to the act of revelation. One feels it especially when one looks at the great blazing suns he painted. His sun was an ominous, destructive vitality; it hangs over his landscape like a symbol of wrath and consumes the very objects to which it imparts a fleeting life. In some of his better moments Chaplin too expresses this feeling. The little clown,the vagabond, the insouciant dreamer of life reclining in a huge seashell with a buttercup in his mouth. It is like a solemn caricature of the *Primavera* with its false springtime. For Botticelli's spring, like Chaplin's, is a reminiscent spring. Botticelli's world, like ours, was a nightmare. The *Primavera* is a dream of spring: the loveliness of the human body is exposed as a protest as a protest against the foul, black spirit of the monks. And so it is with Chaplin at times: reclining on his elbow in the hollow of the seashell he reveals to us a realm which is the wildest opposite of all that we are able to conceive. And so we laugh. We laugh because it is sheer dream and wish. It is almost sacrilegious. Too unreal to inspire any emotional save ridicule.

What Chaplin has revealed to us is the nullification of the individual. The disproportion between event and fatality is crushing. In the figure of the clown one sees the man of today moving amidst them as in a nightmare. Buildings are no longer places of shelter or protection; the home no longer guards the sacred fire. *There is no hearth:* the buildings have become alive, breathing monster s whose insides are equipped with the most cunning mechanical contrivances for torturing the harassed souls of their occupants. What is the significance of these mad chases through houses littered with bric-a-brac? What does it mean—these dream-like pursuits in which the stairs give way and the floor opens up like the bottomless pit? Is it not a symbolical picture of the Inferno which man has created for himself on earth? And where does Chaplin put his Inferno? In the home, in the sacred place of retreat which man built as a refuge and protection against the evil forces of the outside world.

There is something about Chaplin and about Van Gogh which is terrifying. It is their sincerity, their earnestness. The absurd amount of passion with which Chaplin invests his most trifling gestures has a most potent symbolic force. It is the despairing frenzy with which he seizes on things that makes his gestures profoundly grotesque. There is something similarly grotesque, similarly pathetic and ridiculous in the earnest, frenzied gestures of Van Gogh. His objects, whether animate or inanimate, have a luminous, tortured aspect which, in the beginning, made his genius suspect. His objects breathe and twist on a frontier that divides the world of clowns from the world of madmen. Everything is deformed by this inner frenzy, this mad yearning to possess what can no longer be possessed. It is a hunger and a panic at the same time. These men, all of them—Chaplin, Van Gogh, Dostoievski, Lawrence—one feels that they are consumed by the disintegration of the world. Nothing they say quite hits the mark. Everything goes amiss: every dart aimed at the target glances aside, falls quivering into the earth and turns to rust or mold.

Long ago this dread came over man. If one looks at the pictures of Hieronymus Bosch one will be amazed at the modernity of them. His Infernos too are equipped with mechanical paraphernalia, with pulleys and trapdoors. It is like a prophetic vision of an age to come. Even in an early American writer like Poe, situated supposedly in a virgin soil, amidst a pioneer people, there is this same presentiment of approaching doom. In Poe the *object* is haunted; the human figure sleeps or walks somnambulistically, the houses are evil, diabolical traps in which the soul of man is tortured and finally crushed. With Dostoievski the demons are unloosed, the spirit utterly mad, possessed. Man moves against the background of Nature hallucinated, a being entranced and without reason. Nature retreats more and more. The background fades out steadily, until by the time we come to Proust Nature is completely disintegrated and intellectually analyzed. People speak of the great beauty of Proust's descriptions, his marvelous delineation of natural phenomena—but it seems overlooked that they are marvelous *intellectual* descriptions. His landscapes, his flowers, his sky, his ocean are all in the head, all *interior* paintings, all done blindfolded. They are *reminiscent* studies, *reminiscent* portraits, *reminiscent* paintings. All woven out of regret, out of melancholy and yearning. Proust has given us the most wonderful mausoleum of Nature; all the objects which his vision had once cherished are preserved in wax under a glass bell. Never is there a careless, an insouciant touch. No flower is allowed to perish, no sky permitted to fade. Everything is preserved with infinite care, infinite pains—so as to live on in death forever.

When one is a hero to himself he feels under no obligations to do things. He just is. And so one goes through life with a heavily increasing remainder. One accumulates the heroic in himself by allotting to others their possibilities. To accuse the artist of not living because he does not act in the height of ignorance. The man who would live out his multitudinous lives has no time or place in which to act. Action destroys all but what is known as one's life. Based on the theory of "the one and only" life always tends to assume a sacrosanct quality.

The dream acquires its true significance for us only when the human organism is diseased. The normal man is not supposed to have any dream life, and the proof that he doesn't have any is that he doesn't remember any. He is a hundred percent human, or animal. This fascination for the animal side of our nature leads us to ignore, or despise, the plant in us. This aspect of life is explained away by the vegetative nervous system which we have invented, just as we have invented the locomotive. The dream side of life, which the plant glorifies, gets pigeonholed through our singular vision of things as morbid phenomena. The human side of life is the waking side. All the progress we have made is chalked up on this side.

If man is ever going to become himself, MAN, and not something different, he will have to stand outside the realm of Idea and, growing more and more satisfied with himself, vegetate. He will have to admit that the dream of the idle weed, which produces only its kind, is closer to the miraculous than the most miraculous dream of evolution. He will have to take the miraculous more miraculously.

My plan, then, in so far as the negation of all effort and purpose may be said to be a plan, is to stop evolving, to remain what I am and to become more and more only what I am—that is, to become more miraculous. The flaw behind every system of thought, this one included, is that eventually, like the tapeworm, it devours itself. With the weed it is different. The weed exists only to fill the waste spaces left by cultivated areas. It grows between, among other things. The lily is beautiful, the cabbage is provender, the poppy is maddening— but the weed is a rank growth whose only human value is symbolic: *it points a moral.*

Only now, since I have come to some dim understanding of myself, has it become imperative for me to read Dante. My time for reading is short, limited. I don't want to keep informed, or abreast of the times. I have time now only to reread my favorites *and* to taste the flavor of those whom I deliberately and sedulously ignored hitherto. Now I want to read Dante! I want to give him the acid test. I don't ever care to know Occam, or Virgil and his damned Eclogues, or Plato, or Spinoza. I am becoming more prejudiced, instead of less. I grow more ignorant every day—purposely so! I haven't the time to spread myself thin over five thousand years of the past. *I know now what cup I want to drink from.*

All this is preliminary to what I have to say about myself. This is where I talk about myself, *I the Human Being*, born of God and living on the earth, one among a multitude. This morning I was listening to Segovia: he brought me a message from God, via Bach. Every morning he brings Him to me: He comes on muted strings, a flurry of snowflakes, a dash of raw oatmeal. The whole cosmos sings, like a banjo whirling through the ether.

To be able to feed on God is an economic luxury which only the rich in spirit can afford. From this point of view I am a spiritual Asterbilt. I have been indulgenced for a happy death and the way of the cross.

What I believe in with my whole heart is moderation—*for others.* Balance, harmony, proportion—without these the world would go to pot. I try to instill a love of these virtues in others; it makes life easier for me. As for myself, I go the whole hog. What is good for others is not good for me necessarily. The knowledge of that has kept my face smooth and free of wrinkles. I have the placid Apollonian brow, the light glancing in every direction. It keeps me pure at heart, naif, sincere, guileless. I am the innocent one, if ever there were one. The ills of the world are God's affair, not mine. Property, wealth, possessions—these belong to the most powerful. Keep them, I say, and may you have great happiness with them! Without possessions, without world guilt, without sin or evil, I am myself a god. I don't say GOD, mind you, but a god. When I talk of God I put him in caps. That's to show my respect. I get a capital letter—why not God Almighty?

People are, have been, and always will be miserable and restless. There is no cure for this. There are *escapes* only—the "bastard ways," as you say. God is one escape, revolution another, suicide another, madness another, sainthood another. All of these are *lousy* escapes. The best thing, I tell you, is not to try to escape. The best thing is to stick it out. Right now people are going mad: there are no more fire escapes. If the house begins to burn there is no help for it but to jump from the window. *I refuse to jump.* I'm going to sit still and let the house burn down. I'm going to burn down *with the house.*

There's no logic in this. I know it! No dialectic materialism, no race logic, no quantum. This is pure horseshit, without even a drop of holy water to relieve it. But this is the important thing, and if you get this straight, you can forget the rest: *I am singing now while Rome burns.* In order to sing I have to eat every day, and when I eat I get thirsty, and when I drink I get drunk, and when I get drunk, it doesn't matter if Rome burns or doesn't burn, or even if I burn too: I will burn singing—how's that? Or sing burning—that's even better.

If I were a Mary Baker Eddy I would tell you that disease, sorrow, misery, death are figments of the imagination. But I am just a human being, a *healthy* one, and I can tell you safely that this is a goddamned lie. As a plain human being, albeit of a superlative order, I can give you the fullest assurance that there will always be disease, sorrow, misery and death—*if nothing else.* These are not man-made phenomena, thank God, else there might be a possibility of their disappearing some time or another. I didn't discover them—I am merely underlining them. These are the notes which make the diatonic chord, and when struck all together they make the diapason of human woe. When the harp is struck, when it is given a resounding blow, life becomes apoplectically apocalyptic. In other words, Rome has to burn in order for a guy like me to sing.

And so, by whatever route we travel forth, we always come back to the node—myself, a human being, one among a multitude, born of God and identical with Him, suffering the same grief and anguish as the rest, but apart, singing and burning, or burning and singing. In the language of the uninitiated this is called the hocus-pocus of mysticism. It would suit me just as well if the mysticism were left out and it were called plain hocus-pocus. That gives me free rein and a clear field. It eliminates the necessity of competing with other mystics, each of whom has his own hocus-pocus anyway. It puts me in a class by myself, where I belong.

And now I'm going to sing a bit of that "divine entropy" which you failed to grasp in the famous "three pages—how the more we bite into the future the bigger grows the past. The faster the earth dies the more it becomes alive. The earth is only a pin-point and we are something infinitely less. As things grow more impossible what was undreamed of becomes released, *becomes possible*. The only thing that is truly dying off is man's imagination—his ability to dream a new earth, a new heaven, a new hell. We are dreaming, most of us, from the neck up, our bodies securely strapped to the electric chair. To dream a new world is to live it daily, each thought, each glance, each step, each gesture killing and recreating, death always a step in advance. One should act as if the next step were the last, *which it is*.

Nobody knows why anything. Man begins in the womb, a tiny seed. The seed ripens, the foetus drops out—sometimes in a trolley car. Life, however, did not begin in the womb, nor in the seed, nor at the moment of birth. Life is a mystery, and the answer to it is another mystery—*death*. What do I really know, to be absolutely honest? Only that I am alive. Does everybody know that he is alive? No! Some only imagine it: they are looking for proofs all the time. To be alive, *and to know* it! That's almost the sum total. This sound so absolutely trivial I know you're going to skip it. Just the same, it's the highest statement I have to make. What follows will be easy for you and will make you realize that I am just a human being like yourself. To wit . . .

Some of you reading these lines are now lying in bed; some of you will croak tomorrow; some of you have no time to read me because you are begging for a crust of bread. By rights I ought to be doing the same thing—either lying in bed, or croaking, or begging my crust of bread. Happens I'm not. Happens I'm adding an addenda to a book which is already finished. Happens the book doesn't need an addenda, but I must put it in just the same. This is the highest act which a man can perform—to do that which was not expected of him. *To do something gratis*, in other words. If you cotton to that you'll know what kind of guy I am. You'll know that I was born with a silver spoon in my mouth, that I was born with genius and that I had the good sense to cash in on it immediately. Yesterday I was in New York, today I'm in Paris, tomorrow it'll be Shanghai or Singapore. Bound down by the cruelest economic laws a bum with a pocketful of ticker tape. I'm off, sailing, already on the high seas, looking blankly at the horary ocean, my body already in Paris, Shanghai, Hong Kong, Honolulu, Singapore, Nagasaki; walking the streets, beginning a new book, repeating myself, singing, cursing, dancing, whistling, wondering what next. I greet you all, everybody, the Jews of New York, the gangsters in Chicago, the politicians in the White House. I greet all the bedbugs and cockroaches sweating for a living, greet all the radio announcers, the crooners, the sleek advertising gentry, the hoofers and patterers, the handicraft men and the machine gunners, the clerks in the subtreasury vaults, the ditchdiggers, the penpushers, the bus drivers, the traffic cops, the street walkers, the dope peddlers. Greetings! Greetings! I walk out on you with my book under my arm. Almost everything I wanted to say I have left unsaid. It's the human being in me which prevents me from spilling the beans. Don't ask me any questions, because I have no answers. Run with your urine to the Jews. Bring your complexes to the Institute of the Holy Ghost. Save your statistics for Karl Marx. The wise men solves no problems. The wise man says—*it is written in the stars!*—and so saying, he picks up his flute and blows a mournful note.

6

November 26, 1935

If you have followed the inner progression of the preceding pages you will realize that what we are coming to presently is a discussion of "reality."

When I think of Hamlet I think of an Anglo-Saxon in doublet and hose (equipped with a far purse) fighting with a ghost. The ghost of the Absolute. When I think of a Yogi I think of an emaciated Hindu throttled by a ghost. The ghost of the Absolute. Between these two extremes of temperament lies the Chinese realm. To make a little clearer what I am driving at I must go back a bit . . .

It's something like this . . . The world that Copernicus opened up Einstein brings to a close on the fantastic figure of 35,000,000 solar systems, the axis of this incredible system having the immeasurable length of 470,000,000 times the distance from the earth to the sun. (This is progress, as you can see, if only in the domain of calculation.) Anyway, coincident with the collapse of this bubble there emerged the cocky little skeptic, Lawrence, who, with something more like the imagination of a Kepler, throws the whole thing overboard. In place of the myth which science has elaborated, Lawrence struggles to reestablish a more creative, more poetic, more *human* myth, in which ideas are again related to living, and not to dead facts. In *Art and Artist* Otto Rank has pointed out that man originally studied the heavens in order there to read his fate, and of course, to *thwart* it. But what he discovered, Rank emphasizes, was not his fate, but the science of astronomy. This picture of the multiverse has now reached its limits, as has the corollary picture of the atomic multiverse. What commenced in Chaldean times, or earlier, as body projection, with all the dream-sure certitude of organic evolution (as the lore of the zodiac indicates) comes to smash finally upon the old rock of reality. Man is still trying to read his fate, and *to thwart it*, but now he looks within, back through all the layers of dream and myth, through all the myriad strata of the geologic "I." The two pseudo-sciences—astrology and analysis—represent the extreme poles of a constantly changing view of reality which corresponds to our notion of "the world." Between these poetic limits of apprehension arise the changing cultural forms which appear and disappear on the surface of human history. One of these forms, or myths, has now reached the saturation point: the myth of science. The world senses vaguely, but definitely, that things are in a state of transition. The collapse of the world is the collapse of the myth.

The swing outward, the centripetal, the macrocosmic urge, has reached its peak. With the turn of the tide we are swimming back to flood the psychologic gulf, the deep winter marshes in which are stuck the empty symbols of the past. With the enthusiasm of pioneers and discoverers we are bringing to light the flora and fauna of the world to come, a world that will be inhabited by the ghosts of ourselves. To reanimate these dead forms, to give them meaning and value, a religious feeling is imperative. No new Culture rears itself without the prime symbol—soul. What we have at present, even in its most helpful aspect, is not in any way akin to a religious spirit. Our condition is more like that of the disintegrative period of the Greco-Roman world when, sensing the death that was upon them, helpless, desperate, frantic, the peoples of that great civilization fell victim to the shallowest creeds, cults, doctrines, philosophies—anything that promised the stay of the inevitable. It was out of such a bacillic stew of ideas that the regenerative doctrine of Christianity was born. Then as now the keywords were hallucination, dream, mystery, resurrection. Rimbaud rode in on the crest of modernity frothing at the mouth. Dream, hallucination, mystery. *Smash everything!* This, too, is a very real sense of destiny. It is *our* destiny.

Behind the phenomena of human activity lie incalculable forces.

Both astrology and psychoanalysis have for their grand aim the revelation of the extent and magnitude of these forces. The motivating spirit of inquiry is based on the recognition of life as conflict, whether the theatre of conflict be projected outward to the stars or inward to the unknown regions of the Unconscious is relative and secondary. A sense of mystic participation with the universe, a religious awareness, is the all-important. Both views are founded in that older, sounder view of life which Lawrence proclaimed. "Early science," he said, "is a source of the purest and oldest religion.... The very ancient world was entirely religious and godless. While men still live in close physical oneness, an ancient tribal unison in which the individual was hardly separated out, then the tribe lived breast to breast, as it were, with the cosmos, in naked contact with the cosmos, the whole cosmos was alive and in contact with the flesh of man, there was no room for the intrusion of the god idea. It was not until the individual began to feel separated off, not till he fell into awareness of himself, and hence into apartness; not, mythologically, till he ate of the Tree of Knowledge instead of the Tree of Life, and knew himself *apart* and separate, that the conception of a God arose, to intervene between man and the cosmos. The very oldest ideas of man are *purely* religious, and there is no notion of any sort of god or gods. God and gods enter when man has fallen into a sense of separateness and loneliness ... Away behind all the creation myths lies the grand idea that the cosmos *always was*, that it could not have had any beginning, because it always was there and always would be there. It could not have a god to start it, because it was itself all god and all divine, the origin of everything." Now this attitude is precisely the opposite of the scientific, with its insane idea of a conquest over Nature, over the mysterious forces of the universe. Where astrology, for instance, *and* analysis fall short, is precisely in their submission to the inquisitive, scientific spirit. The creative, the *poetic*, aspect which Science shares with all the arts is swamped by the pragmatic. The desire to subjugate the forces of Nature for practical purposes, instead of exploring them in a fictive, a metaphysical, a *disinterested* way, has brought about an empty *knowledge* of Nature, instead of a wisdom of life. Life and death lose their significance, their polarity. In place of the drama we have an empty continuum of work.

Even to early man life presented itself as a problem-situation represented by a closed circle. Life appeared closed, hopeless, fatal. And so it remains—*fundamentally*. Out of each seeming impasse man is lifted by the time movement into another circle, another plane, with different problems, which in turn present themselves as closed and insoluble. There never is any solution to a problem except time. One simply moves on or up or out or down to another plane, into another zodiacal sign, among other clusters, constellations, influences, agglomerates, climates, soil, etc., etc. In each of these situations there is a cosmic setup, a *condition of weather* (usually bad), charged with this or that quality which acts upon the individual in a definite way. And there is always a fixed, obsessional point, a magnetic polestar which is interpreted and differently named in different times. Always there are the two phenomena: type and periocity. It is the story of the earth itself—a planet containing the mysterious sign X which, in its orbital swing, encounters fields of influence which are supposedly the same but which vary as the earth and the whole universe travelling with it constantly moves into new sidereal space. Space—Movement—Time. And the time element determines the character-complex of every situation and the lives bound up with it—the lives of individuals, of beasts, plants, stars, suns and constellations. The sidereal time picture is the constant, just as light is the absolute in physics. We take the picture for granted, examine it no more, because it is relatively fixed. It may last ten thousand years or ten billion years—*or it may dissolve tomorrow*. Our conception of historical destiny is merely the counterpart of our picture of scientific planetary destinies. It is a "counter-concept." We plot, we describe order, we can even prophesy with accuracy—all within a tight, theoretical frame which may last a long time, as long as our history—but where that stops is utter chaos, and the prevision is, always, *catastrophe*.

An artist, in the evolution of his works, which is simply the *historical* record of his changing problems, reveals this cosmic pattern, this obsession. He is not therefore and consequently a magician, an astrologer, or a scientist, or a philosopher, or a moralist, or even a psychologist. The prophetic *and* the musical aspect of the poet's life and world spring from his fluid apprehension of the real nature of changing phenomena. He stands outside all systems of thought—in the quick of a permanent cosmic order, or design. That is why he sings, music being the essence of this unison with reality, this life that is detached from image and idea. And that is why he is prophetic: he has his finger on the cosmic pulse which beats eternal. That is why he is anarchic, because all lesser forms of order must perish to give way to greater, unseen, unknowable order. That is why he sings about life—*how* things seem to him, or *are*. He moves with the spheres evanescent and changing, yet changeless.

In his individual works—and this is more particularly true of the Dionysian type—the artist seems fragmented. But each individual work is a complete representation of his momentary wholeness. The artist lives and dies in each work. His works are a succession of births and deaths, a spiritual progression, a quickening that mocks the slow, torpid life-death or death-life of the mass about. Through his inexhaustible roles he records the changeless ego, through the poem the eternal how of things. He is like the coiled serpent, the snake that swallows its own tail. He consumes himself, and in devouring himself he completes the picture of the world. He is the circle without beginning or end. It is a constant, ceaseless hunger, a desire for union, for oneness, for completion.

This is the only spiritual dynamic he recognizes. A sort of fourth-dimensional state. A continuous exfoliation, a paradoxical intra-extroversion. To put it another way his ambition is to rival the dung-beetle which evacuates in the same measure and the same rhythm as it devours. He eats his way into the ball of dung, which is life, in perfect bliss. The whole organism sings of digestion—a state of "adjustment" beyond any described by the analysts. To him, therefore, the misery which we create for ourselves is brought about solely by our inability to unload the food which we have ingested. We have indigestion and so we build up a picture of the world-as-disease which is "spiritual," with the result that the genuine and very real bellyache of which we suffer gets refined away into a language of imaginary aches and pains for which there is no remedy, except death. What is not fully "experienced"—that is, ingested and excreted—passes off into the poison of knowledge. "To know oneself" becomes the all-important: a false and endless pursuit, a tail-chasing.

In a way, then, the artist is always acting against the time-destiny movement. He is always a-historical. *He accepts* Time absolutely, as Whitman says, in the sense that any way he rolls (with tail in mouth) is *direction;* in the sense that any moment, *every moment*, may be the all; that there is nothing but the present, the eternal here and now, the expanding infinite moment which is flame and song. And when he succeeds in establishing this criterion of passionate experience (which is what Lawrence meant when he spoke of obeying the Holy Ghost inside one) then, and only then, is he asserting his humanness. Then only does he live out his susceptible to all influences—and everything nourishes him. Everything is gravy to him, including what he does *not* understand—*particularly* what he does *not* understand.

This final reality which the artist comes to recognize in his maturity, this China which the analysts situate somewhere between the conscious and the Unconscious is that symbolic paradise of the womb, that pre-natal security and immortality and union with Nature from which we must wrest his freedom. Each time he is spiritually born he dreams of the impossible, the miraculous; dreams he can break the wheel of life and death, avoid the struggle and the drama, the pain and the suffering of life. His poem is the legend wherein he buries himself, wherein he relates of the mysteries of birth and death—*his* reality, *his* experience. He buries himself in his tomb of poem in order to achieve that immortality which is denied him as a physical being.

The artist's dream of the impossible, the miraculous, is simply a result of his inability to adapt himself to what is vulgarly called "reality." He creates, therefore, a reality of his own, in the poem, a reality which is suitable to him, a reality in which he can live out his unconscious desires, wishes, dreams. The poem is the dream made flesh, in a two-fold sense: as work of art, and as life itself, which is a work of art. When he becomes fully conscious of his powers, his role, his destiny, he is an artist and he ceases his struggle with "reality." *He becomes a traitor to the human race.* He creates war because he has become permanently out of step with the rest of humanity. He sits on the doorstep of his mother's womb with his race memories and his incestuous longing and he refuses to budge. Choosing the metaphoric symbols hidden in the ideograph he creates an impossible world out of an incomprehensible language, a lie that enchants and enclaves men. This not because he is incapable of living. On the contrary, his zest for life is so powerful, so exigent, so voracious, that it forces him to kill himself over and over. In this way he creates the legend of himself, the lie wherein he establishes himself as hero and god, the lie wherein he triumphs over life.

Life writes itself in terms of color. The absence of color is an impossibility, a conceptual negative. Black and white do not exist: they have been created artificially. We come from an imaginary white and move towards an imaginary black, traversing all the colors of the spectrum as we pass through life.

Color has three aspects: value, chroma and hue. Life is always reflecting these three aspects of color. The three primary colors— red, yellow, blue—might be regarded as three constants, three absolutes. These three colors which the rainbow, in its span between two infinities, reveals to us, I am choosing arbitrarily to represent thus:

1. Red—Experience
2. Yellow—The Unconscious
3. Blue—Thought Process

Each of these are absolutes unattainable, impossible to isolate. We know nothing but a blending of these three primaries, these absolutes; it is only when they are refracted through the prism of death that we see them separate and distinct. They come and go as a sort of miraculous phenomenon, a mirage. The constant and eternal is the transient, the relative, the infinity of change, the eternality of change. The three primaries are *our* primaries, a color condition that we are born to as inhabitants of the planet earth. There may be other primaries for other planets, other beings. We create no new color. The best we can do is to create values, establish chroma, or intensity. This gives our life its cast, or hue.

Color suggests a wheel, the steady progression from one tone to another, without beginning or end. Red is not nearer an imaginary beginning, nor blue an imaginary end: none of the three primaries are superior or inferior to the other—they are co-existent and rule with equal power. The significance we give to them is human and arbitrary. We have the choice of creating our own values—that is, significant relationships.

As color faces, as it "grays," so to speak, it moves towards a hypothetical black. As color blends, it moves towards an imaginary white, a condition where one tone so neutralizes the other as to produce the illusion of the absence of color.

An idea state of living would be the imaginary one wherein the three primaries prevail. Here the wheel of color confronts the prism of death and gives us the phenomenon, fleeting and recurrent, of the rainbow or spectrum. Life is not seen in terms of changing values, changing intensity—through all its varying hues—but abstracted, arbitrary, false, unstable. The rainbow is a symbol, a revelation—nothing more. In using red to denote the value "experience" I am making the natural association of blood and life. Red has always been a royal color and boldly employed in periods when, as we say, life ran high. The royal purple, said Lawrence, had a lot more red in it than we usually imagine. (Scientists have said that this royal purple closely approximates the color of the menstrual flow.) As our tendency is to reduce the colors of life, to *gray* them, naturally our reds have become very pale. Bear in mind, please, that in order to designate tones as hot or cold we are obliged to draw an imaginary equator around the globe of color, creating two equal hemispheres. Thus, in order to create the proper values for our color scheme we must set off the warm tones against the cold. A spot of vibrant color will equate a large gray area.

If you will keep this last image in mind you will see that it bears a close analogy to the condition of our life today. For the pallid, death-like quality of our general hue, our everyday living and thinking and feeling, we have by contrast strong oppositional spots of vibrant color—combinations of red and yellow which gives us the orange of insanity and violence, or combinations of red and blue giving us the violet of dream life. Our thought-stuff is a faint cobalt on the verge of turning green.

The more intensely life is lived, that is, the more of red it contains, the more blue thought becomes. Ideas tend towards the pure, absolute strength of the primary blue that which is arbitrarily expressed by a shade between the cobalt of the sky and the ultramarine of the sea. The ideational process is fixed, as it were, between the two poles of infinity represented by the womb and the stars. The highest flights of thought always represent this span, this bridge between the microcosm and the macrocosm.

We say about our condition today, very falsely, that it is all thought, when we mean "introspective." What we mean is that the insane intensity which gives to our living its one brilliant spot of orange can only be balanced by an enormous area of blue thought stuff, and very pale blue at that. Where thinking is done it approximates an ultraviolet; that is, the blue and the red mingle strongly, producing the complement to the orange of insanity in the violet of dream. We tend, in other words, to live and think in dream: we are regressing towards the white, or no-color, of prenatal life.

The predominant tone of our physical surroundings verges more and more towards gray and brown, which are not colors, but conditions of impurity, the diminishing, or the muddying, of colors. We are neutralizing in an effort to reach white. Black is liberally employed—to avoid the sensation of color. White is also employed liberally in order to render opaque that which is transparent.

Coincident with the deterioration of the color sense and symbolic of the wish for an absence of all color, is the increasing phenomenon of Daltonism, or colorblindness. This is a condition which is tending to become universal (Dr. Hemingway speaking!)—the inability to see colors any longer, or substitution of one color for another, thus creating a false set of values. This is the condition known as neurosis, whose main characteristic is the loss of tension, loss of polarity. Here it is not so much a condition of loss of color, of graying, as the creation of false color values, so that the primaries are no longer recognizable and the spectrum itself is dislocated, nullified. If the blue is weak it tends to become yellow, a sort of dementia praecox state; if the blue is strong, relatively, it tends to pass over into red, and we have the phenomenon of paranoia. In other words, we get two insane colors, two incurable color diseases: a praecox yellow and a paranoiac red. In the process the yellow of the Unconscious gets poisoned, it dies.

I choose yellow as the color of the Unconscious, because it lies between the two infinities of red and blue, just as life situates itself in its infinitude between the poles of birth and death. One might say of us today that our values are being expressed more and more in yellows, with relation to the three primaries. Synonymous, analogous, homologous, with the Unconscious I make use of such terms as China, dream, instinct, the Id, etc. With blue and red sinking yellow rises.

If we think of life as a symphony of color, and regard the three primary colors as we do keys in music, then we might speak of certain epochs as representing a symphony in blue, or a symphony in yellow, or in red. A symphony in blue would not mean that red or yellow were absent, but that all the colors employed were keyed to the primary one, the dominant blue, for example. At present we are in a state of transition; we are modulating through the subdominant keys, through the feeble grays and the muddy browns, from a dominant blue to a dominant yellow. We have switched from one key to another many times in the course of our history. We have had scarlet periods and vivid blues, and we have high yellows. (The Greeks, for instance, switched during their history from a vivid red to a vivid blue; the Chinese and the Hindus lived out mighty symphonies in yellow.) Our yellow is still faint, but the progression is definitely indicated: *from blue to yellow.*

The green of spring may express itself throughout the whole chromatic scale—of green. A truly vernal green would be composed of an equally strong mixture of blue and of yellow. They would be fresh, warm blues and yellows combining, and the red would be scarlet. Such a vernal green would be characteristic of the spring-time of a great culture; it would differ from the green of a Renaissance by virtue of its warmth. In the latter, a false springtime, we have a strong but cold green, a green tinged with blue.

Our spring, which I have styled a "Black Spring," contains the faintest hue of green. The yellow in it is scarcely felt—it is suffused with blue. This spring consequently, is the palest, weakest, deadest spring it is possible to imagine. It is spring registered in terms of minus.

During this modulation, then, from one color key to another, all values are confused and blurred. Forms are difficult to discern or distinguish, the tempo is rapid and constantly shifting. It is like a photographer turning the lens of his camera in order to get the proper focus. Suspense before the final resolution—to pass over into a different key, the destined key.

Form, in short, is not yet. The forms of life lie below the surface, below visibility—except for the painter whose eyes are trained to detect the slightest nuance. For the latter, an artist already working into the future, there is the need to counterbalance the heavy area of blue in which he has been working by the manipulation, the *frantic* manipulation, I might say, of intense intermediate tones. He is trying, with all his powers, with all his technique, to feel his way into the yellow. For him each feeble spring grows slightly greener, slightly warmer, more vibrant. He is only on the fringe of the yellow. His forms, registered as they are in the palest greens, are scarcely capable of making themselves visible amidst the cloying and obscuring browns and grays in which the old forms are crumbling. Form itself, when he can detect it sufficiently to recognize it as form, has but little significance. There is not yet enough yellow in the sunlight to supply his plant forms with the necessary chlorophyll. They die almost at birth. Birth and death are closely merged: life gets stifled, strangled in the womb. But life is there, at the roots, in the subsoil, and it is the blue seed of thought, of ideation, which nourishes it. The bright sapgreen, the toxic chlorophyll will come—when spring is at the full, in the flood of the tide.

As the significance of the old forms empties itself the significance of the new makes itself felt at the roots. It is *historical* significance, the dying blue warming to the pale yellow, creating the faint green cell forms. Such as Picasso's creation—suffused with dying thought, but carrying the promise of a vernal green. With waning colors no great form is possible. The artist who works exclusively in the key of blue is doomed, however great his ability. In fact, the greater his work, the more disastrous will be its end. Such are the works of Proust and Joyce—monumental edifices in cold, pale blue. Rich tones of brown in Joyce, beautiful melancholy grays in Proust—but their compositions set in the fatal key of blue. Lawrence, on the other hand, with his strong emphasis on the reds, produces the illusion of a warmer green—but it is illusory. His swift modulations and jarring dissonances serve one useful purpose however—they make us more strongly aware of the suspense before the final resolution into a new key. Lawrence brings sharply to our consciousness the agony of the suspense; he dwells on it, as though the suspense, if sharp enough, is sufficiently prolonged, would create of itself the transition to a new key. Against an overwhelming area of cold pale blues he has counterpointed the most intense spots of hot color. His compositions have a strident, clashing dynamic, an overemphasis, with a resulting obscuring and the inevitable accompaniment of false values. But the significance is there: the terrible significance of the old forms and the vague, intuitively sensed significance of the new. The greater part of his energy was used up in killing off the old forms.

The artist has always been invested with a vicarious magic power. But today we realize that the artist has failed to live up to his trust. He has betrayed the powers that be. And in return he has been stripped of his authority, his privileges. His magic no longer works—not because magic has been disproved—but because in him magic is dead. A mighty chasm yawns between him and the mass who once looked to him for authority, for the divine utterance which would bring release. He stands now stripped of power, his voice dried up. What he says is incomprehensible. Perhaps it was always incomprehensible, but in the past this very fact of non-comprehension worked a spell upon the listener. The audience did not ask to understand—men begged to be visited by the demon and then exorcized. Now the artist goes about like a freak, like one who has been visited with the evil eye. He is given crazy, tattered garments and his garments are held together with rotting bones, they are soiled with filth.

An artist like myself, consequently, *a late-city product*, so to speak, twinbrother to Grosz, Whitman, Van Gogh, Strindberg, the brothers

Bosch, all the demonologists, finds himself under a supreme obligation, entrusted with a sacred mission. He must escape this death which is engulfing the world in order to protect and preserve his magic role. He flees to an imaginary China (hasn't the artist always done this?) where the changeless man (changeless only for the last 20,000 years: *Homo Sapiens*) resides. The fundamental, changeless, rock-bottom man, immortal, unscathed by catastrophes. With kaleidoscopic changes of mask he hypnotizes his audience into a superstitious state of mind whence they may proceed from doom to magic once again. Guided on the one side by his brother the criminal, and on the other side by the lunatic whose obsession is to fly away from the earth. The tension between the two poles of destruction preserves in him a peculiar dream equilibrium. His voice is heard above the wrack of doom—*joyous and prophetic*. He seeks not to make himself understood, but to be heard. He vibrates with new pains, new sorrows. He takes the discarded enameled plate left in the desert by a wandering archaeologist and, stringing it with his own guts, covering it with his own skin, he creates a new kind of tympanic music, the Chinese song of the rock-bottom man. It is his passion for singing, *nothing less*, which restores song to the world.

It is impossible for me to detach ideas from the man any more than I can detach man from his time, or my little destiny from the greater destiny of the globe. I am moving in a world of human beings who are profoundly influenced by plant, beast, star, climate, soil, weather. Their ideas interest me profoundly less than the separate elemental factors—soil, climate, star, plant—which gave birth to their ideas.

7

December 16, 1935

As I commence this letter I am reminded of the discussion we had some weeks ago about "dishonesty," concerning which you promised to write me at length. In my mind I am still turning the corner at the Boulevard Saint-Germain and the Rue Bonaparte where, you will remember, I confessed to you later that I began to acquiesce—out of sheer fatigue. In a way I am perpetually turning the corner with you. That is to say, we are always coming to some momentary point of agreement by peripheral collisions.

What disturbs me, with regard to your theory of reminiscent time (the creative memory process), is that you bring the present to a dead point. You call halt! and then, like a Mississippi steamboat, you reverse the paddle wheels and travel backwards down the stream of time at will. You say this is *necessary* because "there is no future ahead." *Not for us*, anyway. And you present this to me as an "artistic solution" purely. It seems to me that what you are attempting here metaphysically is a spiritual somersault which it is impossible to perform. I tried to point out to you last night wherein we differ concerning this standpoint of the "present," which might be defined briefly as an attitude based upon the keen realization of the death which surrounds us. I said simply that this realization was in itself all that is necessary—to give us a sense of life. You seemed to think, if I understood you rightly, that it is necessary to throw oneself back, figuratively speaking, again and again to various points in the past in order to nourish this sense of life. To die over and over again, is the way you put it, I believe. And I asked you—how far back can you go in these "memory deaths?" Can you go back beyond your own life experience? And how? And to what end?

Again and again I have tried to point out to you and to others that while accepting the Spenglerian theory as an historical pattern valid for the description of big movements, I do not accept it as applying to the individual artist. My effort to describe the spiritual adventure with Lawrence has its origin in this point of discord with the great megapolitan maestro. As far as Europe goes, as far as America goes, I am one hundred percent for the Spengler. But when it comes to myself I draw the line. Is this a colossal piece of egotism? Megalomania? I don't care what it is. I have a thousand ways of responding to the overtones of that precious word *Sorgen* which no Frenchman has the slightest inkling of, nor any American, which even the Jew, thoroughly *sorged* though he be, does not share with me. Nevertheless, I do not fit in this historical metaphysic. For me it remains a physic, and not a metaphysic. Like Lawrence I have put myself outside this time. I disown it. I am living in the future, even though by the calendar I may be living three days behind the precise chronological moment.

I share absolutely your fervid desire to relate Hamlet, as symbol, to the modern man. What I absolutely fail to see, however, is how you can dare to make of Hamlet the end-all and be-all, as you seem inclined to do. For me life does not begin with, nor much less end with, Hamlet. I have certain genealogical affinities with him, to be sure. I cannot deny my blood. But it is my perogative, as a man, to renounce my lineage, to break the line, as it were. And this I am doing constantly, with all my powers, all my faculties.

For me, as I said last night, the artistic solution to the impasse in which we find ourselves is to move freely upward and outward from the "present" in all directions, achieving a momentary unity with past, present and future. My whole method of obtaining release lies in my achieved ability to start from any moment in the present and work backward, forward and around ad lib. In thus operating simultaneously on all levels I feel that I am able to accomplish the creative act, which is to take wing and sing. My *point d'appui* is the earth, not some ideological factor. At bottom, I have no attitude. I need none because I feel as fixed as the elements themselves. I am a weathercock, if you like. I don't *make* the weather. I register it by viering this way and that. The weathercock is an eternal as the weather itself. You can't have one without the other.

The weather changes imperceptibly and mysteriously—I lay that down as an axiom. The way I react to the weather has some influence upon the weather, helps to *make* weather, as it were. But we can't change the weather by *willing* it. (Revolution, for example, does not alter the weather: revolution is part of the weather complex.) As artists, our problem is not to make weather or to change the weather, but to *record* the weather. By recording I don't mean putting a box on the front page of the newspaper, reading "fair and warmer." That is what the realistic writers do and that is why they change and disappear as the weather changes and new barometers appear. We are not giving barometrical readings. We are reading poems *viva voce*. Those who have ears to hear give heed. For the rest it is silence, always silence.

In identifying Hamlet with the modern man, in making him the arch-symbol of the thought disease, I should like to make it clear that for myself, at any rate, I do not want to be identified with the "modern" man. *This* modern man Jung has called, and I think rightly, the "pseudo-modern" man. The really modern man, says he, is often to be found among those who call themselves old-fashioned. Let me dwell a little further on Jung's idea—it relates very closely to what we are discussing... "The modern man is solitary of necessity and at all times, for every step towards a fuller consciousness of the present removes him further from his original *'participation mystique'* with the mass of men—from submersion in a common unconsciousness. Every step forward means an act of tearing himself loose from that all-embracing, pristine unconsciousness which claims the bulk of mankind almost entirely. Even in our civilizations the people who form, psychologically speaking, the lowest stratum, live almost as unconsciously as primitive races... Only the man who is modern in our meaning of the term really lives in the present; he alone has a present-day consciousness, and he alone finds that the ways of life which correspond to earlier levels pall upon him. The values and strivings of those past worlds no longer interest him save from the historical standpoint. Thus he has become 'unhistorical' in the deepest sense and has estranged himself from the mass of men who live entirely within the bounds of tradition. Indeed, he is completely modern only when he has come to the very edge of the world, leaving behind him all that has been discarded and outgrown, and acknowledging that he stands before a void out of which all things may grow . . ."

I think you will see from the foregoing that we stand far closer to Hamlet, in the sense of an immediate awareness of the present, in the sense of being truly "solitary," than does the modern man whom you appear to identify with Hamlet. I mean that we stand to Hamlet as Hamlet stood to his age. It was the very exactitude of his relation to the age which permitted Hamlet to exist as a "projection" of the modern man. That very exactitude also permits us to regard him as "projection" of the modern man. That very exactitude also permits us to regard him as "projection" into the past. In short, he was so neatly socketed in time that he burns eternally. The ghost, then, becomes the traditional present, that dead slag of the past which refuses to stay buried, which burrows into the present and corrodes it like a canker. Hamlet is the "solitary" Shakespeare who, at the height of his career, turned his back on the stage and was swallowed up in oblivion. What more marvelous example have we of complete identification with the present than Shakespeare? He lived it out so thoroughly that his identify is completely lost.

"An honest profession of modernity," says Jung, in speaking of the spiritual bankruptcy of modern man, "means voluntarily declaring bankruptcy, taking the vows of poverty and chastity in a new sense, and —what is still more painful—renouncing the halo which history bestows as a mark of its sanction." This *un*historical, this Promethean attitude, has to do, as you well know, with the problem of guilt as related to the creative process. What Jung wishes to say, as I see it, is that the only way in which the artist can atone for his break with tradition, for his "originality," is by the quality of his work. The overwhelming burden of guilt demands a corresponding burden of responsibility. This sense of responsibility is imposed from within, by very virtue of being a creator. Shakespeare himself expressed it when he wrote: "To thine own self be true and it must

follow as the night the day thou canst not then be false to any man."
This was the highest commandment that Christ himself laid
down—a commandment, to be sure, which has never been fulfilled,
hardly understood, in fact. Lawrence re-echoed it when he tried to
explain the significance of the Holy Ghost. Each time this fundamental law was uttered we had an attempt to break the wheel of
history. Each time the voice of authority was driven from without
to within. Each time, however, the law has been broken. It will be
repeated again and broken again and again. There is no issue: it is
a truth which one has to reach through personal experience, and few
are able to enjoy the experience.

Let me return to the distinction I had in mind—between Hamlet
prime, let us say, and the other Hamlets of which there are now God
knows how many thousands. Your desire to travel back over all the
roads with Hamlet is, as I already hinted, in reality nothing more
than a desire to travel back *to* Hamlet, that is, to Hamlet *prime* who
has become dispersed through the course of centuries. In this way
you seek a unity which you imagine yourself to have possessed at
a definite point in the past—not necessarily the year 1613, or
whenever it was that Hamlet was born. Somewhere in your own
past you feel that there was a unity which has been broken, and you
want to restore it. You go out searching for Hamlet, hoping to
encounter him some dark night in a forlorn *bistrot*, if not Hamlet
himself, then his ghost.

8

January 31, 1936 (New York City)

Here I am in the land of Hamlets and Othellos, such Hamlets, such Othellos as Shakespeare never dreamed of. End-Hamlets, to be sure. Skull psychologists. The happy land of Schizophrenia where x always equals y and there is never a remainder but plenty of minus signs.

Arriving in this strange world I felt at once that the whole scene existed for me only as tangible, visible proof of our theories. So forcibly did this impress me that for days I walked about as a ghost, a ghost among ghosts. Only my mind told me that I was experiencing something—my senses, my physical organism was numb, paralyzed. If you pricked me I would not have budged. I was in a trance, a coma. I might say that this pall descended over me almost from the moment that I boarded the Bremen. The whole trip was unreal to a startling degree. My kinsmen, the Germans, were dead too—dead in a somewhat different way from the Americans, as I later discovered. But dead. I ate the most sumptuous meals, drank the most wonderful wines, sat in the most comfortable chairs, tipped with the most nonchalant generosity—all without the slightest sense of participation. I thought to myself, if the boat should get rammed and go down in the dark, even that I shall have no sensation; I won't stir from where I'm standing, I won't make the slightest effort, I am not afraid to die because I know now what death is—it is this which I am now experiencing. And thus death became a part of life, where it truly belongs, and I was able to welcome it. For in all things, it is fear which robs us of realization. Fear drops a curtain before the mind—and the ghost walks.

When I had registered at the hotel and sequestered myself in the little cubbyhole which is the room I became active and talkative in that ghost-like way which is so familiar to you. I, Henry Miller, knew then that I was two. In the morning I took my shower, shaved, shoved the Continental breakfast down my gullet and walked out, in the old manner, to buy the morning paper. The man who I thought had died walked briskly to the office of his agent, carried on an amazingly alert, practical, cunning conversation, shook hands all around and boarded the subway for his next appointment. Henry V. Miller also was a brisk, alert, dynamic individual, a man of affairs, a man well groomed, well starched, but not always well oiled, as they say. Henry V. Miller, in his better moments, was once capable of selling the Brooklyn Bridge. Henry V. Miller was a carapace in which there were securely lodged the most amorphous dreams imaginable. Henry V. Miller was brought up amidst the sight of dead cats lying in the gutter, frozen alley cats from Krausemeyer's Alley. Had also seen dead horses lying still and frozen, their shaggy brown coats stuck to the snow-pile like monkey fur. They were huge bloated horses which always died, it seemed, in the moment of evacuation. The carcasses were wheeled away—but the frozen manure remained. And now and then a patch of fur—a sort of furry brown shadow which melted with the melting snow.

These remembrances belong to my boyhood, to that district adjacent to Greenpoint where, in the long winter evenings, coming out of an illness, I would walk to the pork store with a tin kettle to buy a supply of sauerkraut for the evening meal. Coming down into the flitter of the snowbound street, the air frosty, diamond pointed, alone now for the space of a few blocks, a few moments I would become sharply conscious of the world as something which existed outside and apart from me. I could feel a little germ of consciousness forming, a sort of Brussels sprouts germinating in me, which was later to be myself. I mean it was something like a run in a stocking, something just as recurrent and just as sensuous once you had put the stocking on and run your hand along the run. The dead cats and dead horses filled me with a stiff stark wonder—not a wondering about death, but a wondering as to how these once animate creatures now felt in their cold and stiff death, the death in the gutter, without funeral, without tears. They belonged so definitely to life of the street; that is what then impressed me. I could not imagine anything terrible or horrible about death—but just this quality of lying to one side, seen but not recognized, stiff, cold, of no use, like the snow itself once it had been banked up in the gutter.

Something of this sort came over me again when Paul Rosenfeld telephoned me and began to speak of the manuscript I had left with him. It was exactly, to my mind, as if he were describing a dead horse in the gutter. And it will be a dead horse to him and to the whole American public—if they take it. What is more strange is that of all the manuscripts he might have chosen it was that one about his old neighborhood, about my frozen dream life as a child, which he was talking to me about. He used the words "nadir" and "ascension." These two words, too, came to my ears so unexpectedly that it was as if I were in a thermometer, a little piece of quicksilver shooting frantically up and down, but never able to get outside and say "Stop!" He held me imprisoned, quaky, jittery, though outwardly the voice was calm, mellow, even mellifluous, for I had reached such a feeling of "beyond" that even the sound of my own voice came to me as from another world. The man who was listening and the man who was talking were two entirely different men. The one was reasonable, smooth, pliant, amiable, courteous, generous, philosophic; the other was a raging maniac. The whole course of my life seemed to have led up to the sale of my birthright. I was parting with the crystallized essence of my amorphous dream life—for a mess of pottage. I remember the title, as he was fumbling around trying to identify the manuscript for me. Do you know, I was thinking, whence this title comes? Have you asked yourself that? And then came, like an automatic click, the word "vagina." The word "vagina" Mr. Rosenfeld had found shocking. The maniac was saying—would you rather it had been cunt, Mr. Rosenfeld? But the reasonable man was saying—why yes, if that's all that matters, why put in a dash . . . to be sure . . . certainly. And with that the ghost appeared *"Into the night life seems to be exiled what once ruled during the day."*

This sentence, says Gottfried Benn, contains the entire modern psychology. It is taken from Freud's *Interpretation of Dreams*.

"Into the night life . . ." Not "seems to be" as Freud put it, but *has been* exiled all that once ruled during the day. Just as you learned, in your last six months at the Villa Seurat, to move from the past participle to the imperfect tense of the verb "to die," so Freud should amend his famous key to modern psychology. It is amazing how the American people come to life, both in the waking state and the unconscious state, only as night falls. Those who are awake and walking about become raving maniacs; those who are asleep pass into the nightmare. The old people especially seem to have a holy terror of death. They are the real barflies, not the youngsters. The old here are degenerate to a nauseating extreme. The young are melancholy. The lulling hypnotic radio tunes, cheap as they are, having a tragic quality—for the ear that listens attentively. It is, as Keyserling has so well pointed out, the domination of a whole continent, a whole people, by Nature. No gods have been born, none are even in process of being born. At the Rivoli a Rene Clair picture is being shows—called *The Ghost Goes West*. Yes, the old Glourie Ghost has gone West to haunt the empty bodies of the transplanted souls who now make up this continent. The old Glourie castle is taken apart, stone by stone, and removed to America, but with it, willy-nilly, goes the Ghost. In the ancient coat of armor a radio is installed; in the moat surrounding the castle a gondola is seen to glide by. Nine hundred years of history, of soul-stirring and soul-striving, are obliterated, spat upon, disowned, in the Everglades of Florida where the reconstructed castle rises—but the Ghost will not be laid. The double theme continues—this time in Scottish guise. Rene Clair abandons the true artform bequeathed him by the Surrealists to titivate the American sense of phantasy. The box office is appeased. Europe is denied, vanquished, castrated. Abelard again. Primitivism—false primitivism—versus Culture. The American aboriginal takes to his bosom his own schizophrenic theme and discovers it to be a "delightful ghost story." Next week Charlie Chaplin comes to the Rivoli, at $5.50 a piece, for a seat, in *Modern Times*. A new generation has sprung up since his debut. Charlie Chaplin is dead. Keystone is dead. The silent movie is dead. *Modern*

Times! Already it has an archaeological ring to it. The ghost of Chaplin is trying to make itself heard. The ghost will have a box office success. Chaplin too was taken unawares, in the midst of a deep slumber, and castrated. But for him there never was an Heloise, nor a God for whom he could wage a valiant struggle. Chaplin owes his fame and prestige entirely to the unconscious exploitation of his "night life." HIs world tour was a rude awakening. He lost the faculty of dreaming. He read too many books. And finally he fell into that most disgraceful condition wherein he sought to imitate himself. The man who touched the heart of the world because he seemed, like Christ, to be the most solitary figure in the whole living world, this man whose mask was more real than the living flesh, this man has now been dismembered, dispersed throughout the world. I shall go to see *Modern Times* as I would go to see a Greek tragedy if I were living in the age of Pericles. To me, Chaplin, like Lawrence, symbolizes the tragedy of man versus the times. Lawrence conscious to the nth degree; Chaplin absolutely unconscious. Both victims of the age—the one knowingly, willingly even, the other unknowingly, unwillingly. The maniac in me says: Kill Chaplin! The reasonable man will probably pay $5.50 for a seat in order to weep unseen.

Turning the corner of 57th Street yesterday, in a dreamy mood, a violent gust of wind blows a man's hat into the air and I run to catch it. As I hand it to the owner I recognize the man's face. "It seems to me I know you," I say. "You probably do," he says, "my name's Robinson." Immediately I know who it is I am talking to— our friend, Edward Robinson of *"Toute La Ville En Parle."* I walk with him a little ways, talking of Gaston Madot and Brunel and then he dives into a taxi. A strange *rencontre* which may bear fruit, as I have since written him a letter about the "double" theme. It is not the first strange encounter I have had since I am here. Hiding away as I am I feel that I shall move in a strange reality. I feel that I am going to be ferreted out. The very fact that I no longer have any need of America means that I am a disturbing factor in their midst. "Remember that you are an American," my mother used to say to poor Tante Melia. That phrase has always stuck in my crop. I heard it said to Tante Melia under the most cruel and humiliating circumstances. It aligned me immediately with poor Tante Melia who was helpless, defenseless, who lacked this Americanism which should have saved her from misery. Tante Melia did not know how to wage the ordinary battle against the world. She let the woman from Hamburg enter her home and steal her husband away. Her man, Paul, hanged himself; Uncle Louis made her a cripple with his heavy club foot; the relatives farmed her out, like a slavey. In the thirty years that she's been in the lunatic asylum, Mele has had plenty of time to reflect on that phrase which my mother dropped one day—*remember that you are an American!* I have taken up the cudgels for Mele. Not a day of my life passes but I remember that I am an American. The maniac in me rises up each morning with a bloodcurdling war-whoop—*kill the Americans! Bash their bloody brains in!* Everyday it is a fight against Nature. *America must be destroyed!* But the rostrum is gone, the senate has evaporated. I am left howling in a wilderness, and those I would destroy have already destroyed themselves. "The hereditary patrimony of the middle brain!" These words leap forth out of the night life as I turn toward the "psychological facts." "The scar tissue of the hind brain." Teritiary ... ganglionic ... patrimony ... nadir ... ascension. Little bits of scar tissue floating in the void of Nature. Cultural tidbits, the confetti and the oatmeal of the past. "That story about the nutty Jew ..." says the oily voice of Paul Rosenfeld over the phone. "Distinguished writing." "Nadir." "Ascension." So *what*, dear friend? So *what*? I have come to America to buy *The City of God*, to reread *The Tales of Old Japan*, and look up *The Chinese Written Character* by Ernest Fenollosa. I have come to catch hats when the wind blows. I have come to see *Modern Times* at $5.50 a seat.

9

America is the most wonderful illustration of the analytic situation—except that the analyst is missing. Thinking of the letter I wanted to write you I was compelled to make a note of this phrase which kept repeating itself in my head all day: "How far we are from the world of Andre Breton." This was the clue by which I intended to recapture the complex bundle of emotion which this country inspires in me day after day. In reality all these emotions resolve themselves into one—my joy in realizing that I am free of this country, that I have no need of it, that I can not be dominated over or tyrannized or enslaved by it. That is the real reason why her problems leave me unaffected. It is not hatred of it (for if it were I should have cause to feel uneasy), but indifference. I lived out my American problem; it is for the other 120,000,000 Americans to live out theirs.

Perhaps that is the reason why Andre Breton's name came to my lips, for with it is irrevocably associated the word "super-reality." Whatever else it may mean super-reality is not this which passes here for reality. No matter how taut this reality becomes, no matter how ludicrous, tragic, or ridiculous, the most it can become, or the least, will never in the faintest resemble the reality in which the mind of Andre Breton is perpetually swimming. There is an abyss between these two realities, and I know of no bridge which can span them except a wholly new order of experience. That is why I remarked above that America so wonderfully illustrates the analytic situation. By comparison with that other world of which Andre

Breton is a native America is a far-flung empire of neurosis. Her inhabitants are fear-driven dwarfs or giants. The expression of every impulse is negative, critical, analytical. *Or* violent, destructive, anarchic.

It's just a month ago that I started this letter. Since then I have read "The Genesis of Hamlet" by a Yale professor, written in 1902, before the irruption of the psychoanalytic jargon. I see that there were three main sources for Shakespeare's plundering, blundering play. The earliest one was a novel by a Frenchman, Belleforest; then there was a lost manuscript by an Englishman named Kyd; also a poor German play. The problem, as the professor sees it, seems to revolve about the question of whether Hamlet had a weak character or a strong character. When I put the book down I had the feeling which I have always had—that Hamlet had *no* character, that he was a hodgepodge, a composite, and that the grand mystery which envelops the play and makes it a thorn in the side of every succeeding critic, every age, is not a mystery born of Hamlet's character but a mystery created by Shakespeare's bungling. Once again I must try to explain my instinctive aversion to Shakespeare. It has to do with the question of creativity. The business of re-creation has never appealed to me. It's a secondhand way of revealing one's genius. Shakespeare, it seems to me, was an opportunist; were he living today he would be writing scenarios for Hollywood. He would be a glorified Sabatini. Instead of heightening the old material he dilutes it, spreads it thin. It's no accident that he is universally accepted, universally appreciated. The same is not true of Goethe or of Dante. It is more true of Cervantes and Dickens, however. The pantheon of universal types which he created has always had something of the quality of a wax museum for me. Take away the sound and the fury and you have on your hands a fine collection of puppets. No, Shakespeare to me is a great fraud, despite Goethe's enthusiasm, despite the almost universal acceptance of him. I don't like men who strike the norm, who give us universal types, who borrow their plots, who recreate old legends, who kill themselves keeping the market glutted. In short, Shakespeare was definitely not a Surrealiste.

You will recall that this Hamlet theme which now engages us was preceded by a barrage of letters in which I attacked you personally. I told you openly that I was deliberately shifting the ground of our endless discussion in order to reach up inside you with bare hands and gently disarrange your bowels. I didn't fall on you in the dark with a cleaver or a dirk. Like Hitler I simply moved up my men and ammunitions into the demilitarized zone, holding out the dove of peace on the point of my bayonet. I wanted a sovereign equality—not for a twenty-five year peace pact, which is sheer claptrap, but to be able to grapple with you on more equal terms. You had all the advantages of neurosis, of disease—the bacterial equipment, so to speak. I had only my German blood, my faith, my health, my illusions, my ability to die.

My problem is not, and never has been, "to find a solution to Hamlet," as you put it in your last letter. That's *your* problem, inasmuch as you've identified yourself with Hamlet. When I read the professor's book on *Hamlet* in New York I read it to be entertained. The subject of Hamlet *entertains* me, I want you to get that straight. Ideas in general *entertain* me: I don't fight or die for them! I didn't expect, when I opened the book on *Hamlet* in New York, to find a solution to this problem because I understand too well that all these so-called solutions, or attempts at solution, are only meant to broaden or deepen or complicate the problem. What I gathered from my reading of the book is simply this, that Hamlet, like Oedipus, like the Sphinx, represents an eternal human problem which happened to become its most sensational and lasting expression in Shakespeare's rendition of it. I wish I could recall now the difference in thematic detail between the various versions which the professor analyzed and compared. That would be interesting because I should then be able to tell you why I prefer the crude French version of the story to Shakespeare's. I have a poor memory for details, especially where they relate to ideas. I remember only my feelings. My feeling was, and still is, that the French version, which was in the form of a novel, was better. Had there been only this French *Hamlet* I am quite ready to agree with you, and with the world the story of Hamlet would have died. Shakespeare made an enduring myth of it. But in the process he laid the ghost, as it were. Shakespeare killed the problem! He killed it by making it acceptable to the understanding of man. In short, once it fell into the psychological pattern it ceased to become a problem and became a myth. Your attempts to revive the problem are only futile attempts to revive a feeling which is no longer possible, or if not a feeling, an attitude towards life. You want to travel back along a road which is closed. If it were that the road were closed because of repairs only there might be some excuse, some reason in your method. But this is a road which is *permanently closed*. You tell me that the solution to the problem is within myself—as though I didn't know it! My dear fellow, do *you* know it? That's what I wish to ask. Don't tell me, please, that in swimming upstream you are travelling towards the source. When the salmon swim upstream it's for a very good reason. They swim upstream in order to spawn—at least so I'm told. I'm no ichthyologist. What happens, of course, is that they die. But the egg lives on. Now if you wish to say that in this process of dying you had on the spiritual *egg*, your Hamlet, why I can see some sense in it. But then you shouldn't ask me to take your argument seriously. You shouldn't talk about your *solution* to a problem. Or rather, you should talk about the solution to *your* problem. And just what is *your* problem, may I ask? To find Hamlet? To strike a Shakespearean attitude—or a pre-Shakespearean attitude? The problem is in the womb, me boy, and that's why the road is permanently closed. I don't ask you to get right with the world, in that smart aleck American way you imagine, but I ask you to get right with yourself. You believe, if I understand you rightly, that since Hamlet's time we've travelled the wrong road. And you want to get back on the right road. But I ask you—why since *Hamlet's* time? I can see that we've travelled the wrong road since time began. And the reason it's the wrong road is because the element of choice is so obscure. Inwardly we may travel the right road; outwardly our feet wander and we go astray. We travel in swarms, in armies, like the bees and the ants. Outwardly, at least. This road we're always talking about (which is always the right road) is the road to God. Shakespeare didn't open it up, nor Spinoza, nor Plato, nor any one man. Plato, Spinoza, Shakespeare, all these illustrious fellows simply *travelled* along with royal road. (I want you to understand here and now that it was never "the straight and narrow path" but a *royal* road, and there was always the best of company along it.) We may take pride, like the Romans, in our road-making ability, but I have the conviction that the good roads, the best roads, were laid down and from the beginning and exist eternally. And the reason I feel convinced of this—*feel*, you notice—is because when you travel towards God you travel with the wings of angels. The roads are uncharted, but the sense of direction is safe, secure. And so, even when I make a voyage to America, a voyage against my better judgement, I arrive nevertheless a little nearer to God. I come back with St. Augustine and Emerson, not with swagger and boodle. I come back, not to find Hamlet, but to realize a bigger portion of myself. You think I want to whip you into line, to make a hundred percent American of you. In the first place you never were an American, and it's even questionable whether I ever was. (But I had an American problem, just the same!) As to whipping you into line, where's the line? *what line?* I ask. The line you toe and heel, you mean? That's a chalk line. The chalk lines I leave to the geometricians of the soul.

10

May 7, 1936

W hat interests me profoundly in your last epistle is the second paragraph from the last—"only personal biography remains..." Here, though you will never acknowledge it, is the bog in which you lie perpetually ensnared: *the bog of truth*. This truth-seeking, even though it results at last in the discovery of such a noble instrument as the self, is a source of evil. This is the seesaw which makes Hamlet and all the other earnest devils of conscience run amok. The truth will always exist without just as within, and beside truth untruth, perpetually, like Siamese twins.

To revive the Hamlet within you! Curious, how the other night in looking at the film, *Midsummer Night's Dream*, I felt much closer to Shakespeare than ever before. I came home and turned to your *Encyclopaedia Britannica* to discover a little about the genesis of the play and when exactly it was written. I learned practically nothing. What prompted me was a conviction that this must have been written when Shakespeare was at his prime in a moment of full affluence, of health, success and well-being. Here was a surrealistic paean to the night life, a rollicking, reckless tribute to the powers of the Unconscious. Here the poet stepped forth again—*to prove nothing*. A free fantasia in which even Bottom fails to point a moral. And such a jumble! The idiotic Duke of Athens, the English Greeks, the false columns, the whole decor borrowed from a handbook of history for children. Of them all I liked Oberon the best. Oberon the night rider! He comes forward through the gloom of the brake clad like one of the black knights in the Arthurian legends. Behind him the billowing batwings, the smoke and doom, the ghostly web-like touch of dream, the rigid germination of the mineral, the inexorable quality of desire, of desire stronger than will, of dream above life and of life always two-fold. Oberon is a nightrider and his realm is mist and fog, the realm beyond truth, the wild lair of the poet's heard barking like a mad dog—and then it is that I recognize him and accept him.

This is the first time in my life that I enjoyed a Shakespearean spectacle, and I know now why. It is because I was just able to ignore the words. For when Shakespeare talks it is empty prattle to me, but when he nods, when he dreams, then do I follow him—and with a vengeance. Here we leave the realm of truth and moral to enter the realm of music—the only realm of man's which is truly satisfying, complete in itself and requiring no interpretation. This is a seeing into the heart of things with eyes shut. You close your eyes and you put your finger on a stop—anywhere—and then, because of a vibration inaccessible to the understanding of man, millions of other stops suddenly spring up out of the brake of the Unconscious and beg you to put your finger down again, only this time not *anywhere*, but definitely *somewhere*, not necessarily three steps removed, not necessarily according to the curvature of the earth, but somewhere very definitely which will be in accordance with whim whose master is the sternest of all masters. From this impalpable pressure of the fingertips it results that all the secrets of the heart which logic had stopped now pour out and inundate the world. You were talking about truth, it being now within and now without—Hamlet dead, Hamlet revived, Hamlet venerated, Hamlet desecrated. But now as every organ stop bowels forth its secrets there comes about a limitless confusion in which truth and untruth are drowned, and in the surrender to the flux, to the welter of eternal transformation, there is born at the same time an illogical harmony and agreement which simply says—I AM. To the brink of this abyss Hamlet refused to draw near. Tightly and proudly he held himself— held back the gift of surrender. And in this knot of defiance to the flux there was born another melody, the melody of the hollow skull sounding sweet as stench and crystal clear. Poised above the abyss of life-and-death, eternally suspended like a marsh vapor above the stagnant waters, hangs the Absolute, the fruit of all the rotting Hamlets that ever lived and croaked. Here no Puck, no Titania, no Oberon. Not even the idiotic Duke of Athens. Here Thought, lying on its back, pisses forth a perpetual poison. Here the dream is strangled, suffocated. No feet to run with, no hands to grasp with, no voice to shout with. A shuffle, a gesture, an echo. *Hamlet*, for instance, ceased to be *Hamlet* the moment Shakespeare had finished the writing of it. I mean that even before it was produced it had begun to undergo the transformations and permutations which life imposes on everything which is born and dies. A living and a dying at once. Whatever *Hamlet* was, in Shakespeare's mind, perished the moment he had put Finis to the play. Or should I say rather that the uterine Hamlet died? The idea of Hamlet lives on perpetually, changing not only with the times but with each individual who reads it. In order, however, for Hamlet to be born and to lead an immortal life the original Hamlet, *the idea*, I might say, had to die. The idea of Hamlet was nothing more than a fecundating power and the leaven of this idea could only be established through birth, through the imperfect expression of the Hamlet idea which Shakespeare gives us through his play. Hamlet was undoubtedly a hero to himself, and for every Hamlet born the only true course to pursue is the very course which Shakespeare describes. But the question, it seems to me, is this: are we *born* Hamlets? Were *you* born Hamlet? Or did you not rather create the type in yourself? And whether this be so or not, what seems infinitely more important is—why revert to the myth? Here I want to touch upon something which I have mentioned previously, but more cursorily perhaps—this idea of the myth. When at the end of my prefatory letter to *Bastard Death* I said: "We have entered into the creation of a myth," I meant to imply that all this ideational rubbish out of which our world has erected its cultural edifice is now, by a critical irony, being given its poetic immolation, its mythos, through a kind of writing which, because of it is *of* the disease and therefore *beyond* clears the ground for fresh superstructures. (In my own mind the thought of "fresh superstructures" is abhorrent, but this is merely the awareness of a process and not the process itself.) Actually, in process, I believe with each line I write that I am scouring the womb. Behind this process lies the idea not of "edifice" and "superstructure," which is culture and hence false, but of continuous birth, renewal, life, life. And yet it is out of life itself that the idea of death is born, which, to give it a name, is the lying cultural mask. It is this lying cultural mask which you call the "day face" of the world and which you would kill off by denial. This is a religious problem for in essence it means the pursuit of life everlasting, it means the desire to anchor oneself securely in the permanent flux, which in itself is absurd.

There comes a moment of illumination and then they promptly fall back into the Styx. Now you may promptly say, and perhaps with justice, that it is their own and proper fault. But what if you yourself fall back into the Styx? If, instead of *creating* the myth you yourself become a myth? If, confounding subject and object, you raise yourself in ghost-like immortality to sit in eternal judgment upon your work? The function and purpose of myth, I believe, is solely to liberate man from the thralldom of obsession. It is in order to become dispossessed of those ideas which have outlived their tyranny, which have become merely obsessive. Dali, to take a contemporary figure, is a good example of a type who is obsessed. However brilliant may be his expression there hovers about his work the aura of a realm which he has rejected, not through choice, but through blindness. The purely personal, admirable as it is, takes on the fictitious glamour of impersonality. He makes his entry into art by a trapdoor. But he is definitely in it; his hands are black. The work is not immaculately conceived. What those whom we regard as "pure" have tried to convey to us through their fight against art is this—that they have not tried to exploit their talent. One is an artist the moment he is free, for then he can be *possessed*. Then he is free to possess, which is the opposite of having possessions. And by possession I mean not only material things, but ideas, principles, beliefs, etc. To be obsessed on the other hand, means to long to be free; it means a constant and fruitless warfare against the tyranny of things, ideas, principles, loyalties, beliefs, etc. When these tyrannical ideas or possessions are recognized as mythical we are done with them once and for all. They are then relegated to the limbo of god-like things, which means that we at last recognize their significance and purpose in life, or *to* life. Then they are truly dead and we can put Finis to them. They enter the permanent museum of the mind; they grace the living and shine upon us metaphorically.

In the myth there is no life for us. Only the myth lives in the myth. In saying this I have in mind this, that what irritates us so about the living is this fruitless desire to live in the myth, instead of the desire to *create* the myth. This ability to produce the myth is born out of awareness, out of ever-increasing consciousness. That is why, in speaking of the schizophrenic character of our age, I said—"until the process is completed the belly of the world shall be the Third Eye." Now, just what did I mean by that? What could I mean except that from this intellectual world in which we are swimming there must body forth a new world; but this new world can only be bodied forth in so far as it is *conceived*. And to conceive there must first be desire, which is the religious way of looking upon life. Desire is instinctual and holy: it is only through desire that we bring about the "immaculate conception."

II

Y our problem, it seems to me, is not the Hamlet problem, but the ancestral problem. This goes back to a letter which once perturbed you a great deal—because you regarded it as a "personal attack." But my dear chap, it is inevitable that we come back to the attack and to the purely personal. You are trying to make a cosmogony of your suffering. You are taking us in. But I refuse to be taken in any longer. I come back to what I said before we launched this ubiquitous discussion. I will not quote from that letter because after all I have still a little delicacy. But I am not going to be bogged by your parallelopiped ruminations a la Lawrence, by your pretended identification with the spirit of a man who has your exact antithesis in life. The real Lawrence emerged only at that point where you depart from his views. To put it another way, more pointed and more brutal, if you like, I might say that you parted company spiritually by the way you set your faces. Lawrence debouched into life. You debouched into reminiscence. No man of our time felt so keenly as Lawrence the splendor and the magnificence of the past. *Twilight in Italy* is an eloquent testimonial to that. But Lawrence did succeed in severing the past; it was only as men clung to the past that he was saddened and felt the death of the world, a death which he symbolized in terms of grayness, of opacity, of that intermediary realm which the English word twilight so beautifully conveys. Before him Nietzsche had employed it, and Wagner, and Dante too, though with the latter it was the still more significant word Purgatory. Wherever you go, wherever you make your bed, you carry with you the taint and corrosion of your Purgatory. Hamlet was another Purgatorial soul, with no possibility of egress into Paradise. Maybe that's why dear Gertrude had to be slain! As Lawrence has well said—and here I draw entirely different conclusions than you from the words—"the women-murders only represent some ultimate judgement in his own soul." The women-murderers! God bless them! say I. May they murder the whole bloody crew of idealistic males! An end to them! "Mental creatures. Anti-physical. Anti-sensual." You would like me to believe that Hamlet is the summation of the modern problem. "We shall never prove more modern than he," you say. Well, I refuse to be regarded as a modern. Make your definition and die with it. I walk out on you. Whether I am modern, medieval or ancient is none of my concern. I want to be simply a *man*, and fuck the ideal self, the supreme self, the King and the father combined. Fuck them all! I don't understand it any more. I don't want to understand it! "We are of this time, of the time of the earth," says my friend Saroyan. That's good enough for me. Any time, so long as it's of the earth, and no ghosts about. If there be an ancestral curse I am unaware of it. If there be problems I disown them. If I take the trouble to write you it's because it's no trouble at all . . . it's a pleasure. My stomach is filled, I have cigarettes, and the sun is streaming through the windows. What more do you want? One life, and make the most of it! To you that may have a desperate ring, but I assure you I am not desperate. Death is there waiting for me, and when He comes I shall embrace Him. It must be wonderful too to be dead. I don't know what it means yet—to be dead. It's only a way we have of talking. But I believe in it, as I believe in everything. And there's no question in my mind of whether I am dead-alive or alive-dead. Alive, dead—they're just words to me. It's *today* that's all I know, and by Christ it's a wonderful day . . . and tomorrow may be still more wonderful, or worse—who cares? And if you ask me why it's such a wonderful day today I can only say because it's today and that I am of it and in it and there is no yesterday and no tomorrow. Tomorrow I may be what you call dead. So what, *moncher ami*, so what? Today I regard it as a crime even to entertain such thoughts as Hamlet and Orestes. Orestes *was*, Hamlet *was*, but in our words about them we are not. Hamlet had a real conflict and he solved it, after a fashion. A bloody mess it was, the solution, but a solution nevertheless. It brought down the curtain. *You* have a conflict but you don't move towards any solution of it. You deck it out with terminologies, with names, with this and that. *Out with it!* I say. Bring it into the open, into the daylight. Smash it like a louse under the glass. Spit on it. Dance on it. But don't throw out smoke screens. You have been bathing us now for a long time in the fuliginous light of your mental masturbations. We don't know yet who Mathilda was, or why. You tell us everything— and nothing. You are a fancy weathercock, but the weather is always bad. It must be *your* fault, for just plain common sense tells me that the weather changes now and then, that it gets better, or worse. Today it's fair weather and everything is merry and bright. Are you aware of it? What excuse are you making to yourself for this beautiful fair weather, this sunshine, this full breath of spring? Listen, are you up in your attic praying for rain? How do you stand today with regards to the weather? Can't you feel the great change? Or are you still on the other side of life? And *what* life, pray? What does that mean—*the other side of life?* I know only one life, the life of here and now. If there is any other life I can get it only by proxy, as it were. And in the final analysis it doesn't make a bit of difference to me whether that *other life* is or was good or bad, beautiful or ugly. There is only this one life, which is my life, and if it pans out badly it's my own fault. The other day I was miserable, and I told you so. I told you why, and I think it frightened you a little bit—because it reminded you undoubtedly of unpleasant things in your past. Today we eat. After I eat I will digest, and after that I will awoke, and after I smoke I will take a nap, and like that the day will go, one thing after another, each in its turn. *That's today . . .*

12

June 19, 1936

The delay in answering your last letter has been purely "physiological," as you might say. A word by the way, which you seem to misuse. You say, for example, that you fail to understand my letter of May 7th, a superb letter if I must say so myself, and one in which I was never more clear. At my physiological best I am always clear as a bell. And it is always when I am at my best that you fail to understand me. The reason for this is the same reason why you seem to have the impression that we have not yet come to grips, either with each other, or with our subject. Neither of this is true. We have come to grips time and again, and whether we want to or not the subject is always there. The reason why we set ourselves a thousand pages, I must hasten to remind you—for there is a typical error here which you are often prone to make—was because the idea of one thousand, and not a page more or less, fascinated us. As far as grappling with the subject goes we might have disposed of the matter in 200 pages, or less. I might even remind you that you once suggested that we make it ten thousand pages—or do you forget that? It was the idea that we were *not* going to solve any problems which intrigued us. Could there be a solution to the Hamlet problem? Would it not be absurd to entertain such a hope? No, loath though I am to correct you publicly, I must insist that the animating spirit behind this adventure was one of play, of joy and freedom. As to being understood, either by each other or by the public, even that we had tacitly sponged off.

All this, however, has nothing to do with the fact that now and then I succeed in making myself understood, and you likewise. The fundamental difference between us resides in this, that you *will* insist on bringing things to a conclusion. It's your marvelous analytic mind which will not rest content until the subject has been torn to tatters. This is your way of seizing upon things. You must take it between your fingers, metaphorically speaking, and rend it to bits. You are like a savage who takes the watch apart to find out what makes it go, but like the savage again you neither find out what makes it go nor can you put the watch together again. You are left with a beautiful piece of destruction on your hands—a capable job but to what avail? Listen, *must* we know what makes the watch go? Isn't it enough to know what time it is? And does it matter much what time it is? Do we need exact time, railroad time, astronomic time? Or rather don't we wish to forget time and what makes it too?

I must echo what I said in my recent letters—I don't give a fuck whether I am understood in part or in toto. I write to give expression to what I feel. If I make myself understood, so much the better. The being understood is a by-product. I don't write to be understood. I write to make myself felt as a force, to communicate too, if you like. But principally I write out of the sheer joy of writing. I have enough confidence in the processes of the universe to know that eventually everything will be understood. So, for example, when you refer to the poet—"Alas! This is not all of me, only a small part, a word, a word out of this living body"—I don't feel that anything is lost or gained here, so far as understanding goes. To attempt to say the whole self as you put it, is sheer insanity. It is again a grasping at the absolute, at a bogey of the mind. The worst reproach I have to make against you, in this connection, is that you always imply that the only valid form of communication is your own. You are for ice-cold clarity which, I admit, is one kind of communication, or permits of one kind of communication. I don't care a hang about clarity, as you well know. That is, I don't start out with clarity in mind. Now and then I reach those ice-cold regions of the mind and while it lasts it pleases me well enough. But it's not the end-all and be-all. The important thing, for me at least, is to say what one has to say and say it, whether it's clear or not clear. *Is that clear?* As I said a moment ago, my confidence in nature, in human beings, allows me to dispense with a lot of superficial worrying. I am the exact opposite of Hamlet in this respect. I have my moments of doubt, of questioning, of irresolution, but I erect no tragedy on these. These are fundamental elements of the human mind as much as faith and trust, etc. But the parts are never greater than the whole. I am fascinated by the Hamlet problem only because it is so much a part, an integral part, of the human psyche. I accept Hamlet as phenomenon, just as I accept Jesus Christ, or Krishnamurti. Passing phenomena—some more striking than others, some more instructive than others. But passing phenomena just the same. And when it comes time to drop them I can drop them, like hot coals. And I want you to notice right here a peculiar fact about Goethe. Though, being a poet, he gave us only little parts of himself, so to speak, nevertheless in these little parts the whole man always shone through. Nothing is more certain and unshakable, more solid and convincing, than the living words of the man Goethe. Whatever failed to come off, to make itself understood, as it were, never impairs the original spirit. Goethe lives and in him the truth, Goethe's truth, which I understand and accept. Goethe lives in me, not through understanding, but through a magic contagion which the power and the sincerity of the man conveyed through language. There are parts of Goethe which to this day baffle the whole world. They baffled Goethe himself, as you will find, it you read his letters and conversations. But Goethe never doubted himself, nor the efficacy and the value of his words. He had the courage to put down what he himself did not understand, knowing that he was drawing from a divine source which could not fail eventually to make manifest its meaning. This I admire in the good Goethe. What is dark and oracular here bespeaks something beyond the self. The great spirit of the man breaks through the body to ally itself with Nature. Here, thank God, the understanding is at last baffled, at last held in check. If this be *physiologic* expression, then I am all for it. Here I am at home—and I need no understanding.

But you forget something very important. Today I am less a stranger to my own people than ever. I know then now ... I've got the low-down on them. And if I am without a country at least I have found the world. I belong to the wide world now and henceforth, amen! That may be a little hard on America, but it's swell for me. About the cadaver, well, let the dead bury the dead. I don't hold down the hatches. Whatever is in me comes to the surface, sometimes in words, sometimes as gas. Sewer gas, if you like, but what's the difference? The divine afflatus, what is it if not the sewer gas rising from the stinking cadaver of idea?

Knowing what animated me when I wrote the *Tropic of Cancer* (and by the way, I was just entering my forties then, and not my twenties, as you would have it!) I find it difficult to accept an interpretation so original and personal as yours. It's true, I will admit in passing, that hatred and vengeance were the mainspring. But beyond that, for after all that doesn't explain the book, there was the idea of separation. I had to break with the past, my own past particularly. Having accomplished this I no longer felt the need of hatred and of vengeance. Tempermentally I am anything but a meek and humble spirit, you would pretend to make me. My ability to detach myself from ideas and relationships is a sign of moral stamina, of health and strength. I am not less sincere, less human on that account. On the contrary, I am more human, more sincere, since I am always myself. Attachments, whether to ideas or people, cults or traditions, is virtually slavery. I struggle to preserve my freedom. As a matter of fact, it is no great struggle any more, because inwardly I feel free. I change my ideas, my friends, my country as easily almost as I change my underwear. And when they come back from the wash I put them on again and it makes me feel refreshed. Clean linen—there's nothing like it, my boy. Once in a while the laundress slips somebody else's shirt into my laundry. Well, what's to be done about it? If it's my size I wear it. What the hell, a shirt is a shirt, and it's not less a shirt because it has somebody else's initials sewed on it. Personally I don't go in for initials. I always recognize what is mine, with or without initials.

About my direction . . . I've got to draw a line, you say. Either the unabashed thinker or the story teller! Why not both, my dear fellow? Why draw the line? Whether I am what you call a good thinker or not, I do not know. I rather think not, from all you have let drop now and again. But I do know that I am capable of thinking, and of feeling, and of expressing myself. I want to go forward on all fours. I hope never to be a good thinker, like Kant, for example. I hope to be something more than just a good story teller, like Sherwood Anderson, for example. Nor would I be satisfied to be just a Rainer Maria Rilke. On the other hand, unlike yourself, I put up no battle to stand separate and distinct, nothing can prevent it. And as for the "divine jumble," I adore it. I see nothing to be gained by straightening it out. Nothing. I do see, however, that it is part of your nature to want to straighten it out. We need to do that only because we are uneasy inside. We want a little system all our own to explain the works to ourselves. But our system doesn't make the works. Things are constantly falling back into this divine jumble which you inappropriately style Platonism. There is no salvation except to accept the bloody mess, and even then it's not salvation. Of course I am against the known. The known is always false and at least ten years too late. When you say that Knowledge is my great Bugaboo you are absolutely right. But to go on and say that I detest science, metaphysics, religion, etc.—sticking one's finger into the Unknown, as you say—because I might bring up something horrible, *the truth*, that is not true. The fact is that truth is not arrived at that way. The exploration of the unknown yields only the known. We discover only what we set out to find, nothing more. Truth on the other hand comes instantaneously, without search. *Truth* is, as Krishnamurti says. You don't win it. It comes to you as a gift, and to receive it you must be in the proper state. All this is nonsense to you, I know, but I must asseverate it just the same. This is just a piece of mysticism, if you like, which keeps me gay and fit. I may be wrong, but I lose nothing thereby. I am that little particle lost in the body of the world, but a gay capricious one. It's true, I become even a little more gay, a little more capricious, a little more insolent and malevolent, if you wish, when in addition to the state just described, I have also a full stomach. Truth and well-being go hand in hand. Then the bright sword cuts even more brightly. Makes clean separations. Makes for absolution. When we realize that we are truly alone we either go mad or we take to the open road. We are alone, and there's no getting around that. To weep over it is to gather around us the sweet, comforting stuff of the past, the cotton wool of science, religion, metaphysics. I want none of these sweet comforts. The good spring sunshine, the full larder, the sparkling wine, that's quite enough for me. If a friend comes he's welcome. I bid him talk and tell what's in his bowels. I am not less alone because he is there sharing my good cheer. He will go, either presently or a year hence. One comes, another goes. *And yet the world rolls on!* There's something splendid about letting the world roll on even though you have to pass out. What becomes of all the little miseries when you pass on? Who gives a fuck about *your* miseries, *my* miseries? In the knowledge of death everything is perfect, one round globe, a divine jumble with smooth edges, God, man, the beast, the plants, the stars, all one. I wouldn't care if you called it voodooism—it suits me down to the ground. The good thinker who lacks this feeling is nothing but a divine shit after all. And that's what most of the "good thinkers" were. Good thinking I believe in, but good thinking is the prerogative of every man. The good thinkers are a race apart and they leave a bad smell behind them. You think perhaps they penetrated a little further into the unknown than the ordinary fellow? That is a great falsehood. The unknown is a constant and the advances we make into it are illusory. I love the unknown precisely because it is a "beyond," because it *is* impenetrable. To my mind the simple man, the so-called *simple* man, is as capable of making profound observations as the good thinker. The simple man doesn't upset the world, it is true, but he brings a balm, he makes the world more livable. The schizophrenic rush didn't begin with modern man. It comes to apotheosis in him, that's all. In the modern man it gleams translucently.

You beg me to come closer to the heart of our subject. What is our subject if it is not the grievous effect of knowledge? You chose Hamlet as prime symbol and I have no quarrel with the choice. But you know that back of Hamlet stands Socrates and back of Socrates Prometheus, which is to say MAN. Lawrence said somewhere that a horse is always true to its pattern but man you could never rely on, etc. He said that with sadness and distress, something I could never quite appreciate. For at bottom it meant that he did not accept MAN. I should have said man, in small letters, for it was he, Lawrence, who talked a great deal about MAN in capitals. This MAN in capital letters was the ideal man whom Lawrence was seeking to establish, whom no one has yet seen, nor ever will, in my opinion. It was this capital letter MAN whom Lawrence felt he could get along with, could rely on. Poor Lawrence, I pity him for that. The whole race can go to the dogs in this mad search for the ideal MAN. Life goes by too. Everything goes by the board—for what? for a little comfort and assurance. One must fight and fight and fight again, said Lawrence. To what purpose? To establish the kingdom of MAN. Well, the fight was lost long ago. The horse may have his pattern, but he's unaware of it. Man has a pattern, but he seldom lives according to it. Man's pattern is God, but he refuses to recognize it as a creation. The horse is uncreative. He has no god, but he remains a horse all the time. Man oscillates between god and the Devil. He is seldom man. So they say, "they" meaning the bigwigs, the good thinkers. The conflict arises out of the act of creation. Man is a creator. And to create means to destroy at the same time. To destroy usually gives us pleasure, but to create produces a sense of guilt. And why? Because to create entails responsibility. We create out of a sense of insufficiency. Our longing to be understood is only the reflection of our fear of trespassing. A creative act is in the nature of a trespass. It is a violation of the static order of things. We say we want to be understood, but in reality it is the anticipation of war which makes us tremble with you and apprehension. Every creative act is a declaration of war. And war is man's pattern. He hates that which is dead in him, that which is known. Lawrence was divided on this, as we are all more or less divided. His instinct for war was sound; his desire for a kingdom of MAN was unsound.

From the foregoing you can easily see that when the occasion arises I can chop a little logic too. On principle I am against it. For when, for example, I prove Lawrence wrong in respect to certain things I advance neither Lawrence's cause nor my own. Lawrence remains the great individual that he was despite the imperfections which you or I may track down. His quality has nothing to do with the question of right or wrong. What endears him to me is his ability to express himself as completely as he did. I have often said that if I had known him in life I would have found him a cantankerous, pestiferous bugger. I would probably have shunned him, after close acquaintance. But I would never deny him. Any more that I would deny you, pestiferous and cantankerous as you are sometimes. It's precisely because I see you whole that I don't run out on you. If I saw only the human being, or only the thinker or only the poet, if I saw you only in part, as you assert, I might run out on you. But I see you very clearly, in all your parts, and I see the relationship between the parts—even better than you do yourself. The fourth dimensional me that you speak about is the thing one grasps first when one meets a man. It's only because we can attain to that realm, in our intercourse with individuals, that we tolerate them. Otherwise I am afraid it would be quite unbearable. You say I have never smashed the glass, but, that is what I am constantly doing with you, and that's why it hurts. Some day you'll dispense with the mirror altogether and then there will be no more pain—we'll move up right inside your sacred entrails, stir them around with the little index finger and everything will be lovely, hunky dory. Then there will be only one Fraenkel, solid, substantial, indivisible. The water will be squeezed out, just like in the stock market. We'll be dealing only with prime symbols, with the nomenclature of the skeleton, which is your armor, after all. At present you have a fluid quality, a sort of intellectual dropsy. You have a little wheeze too, a physical wheeze which come from too much moisture in the lungs. Get all that sea water out of your system. Give the microbes a chance either to die or to kill you off. I want you to have a clean death, in the flesh, not these anonymous deaths which you enter presumably in microbe fashion. Bring Alfred out into the sunlight and let him gasp his last. Bring Mathilda out too and give her plenty of rope. And finally there's Hamlet—kill Hamlet off too. You've had a long feast on this carrion and it's not done your digestion any good. Nobody can stop you from living your own life. In the past you wanted possessions, security, love, home, all these things which all of us have wanted in our sad, simple way. Now you're dispossessed. You'd almost have me believe you haven't got a friend. You've got the whole world, just for the asking. All you've got to do is to open your trap and take it. Yell for it! Clamor for it! No more death in a room. Make it an outdoor death. Death outdoors! Jesus, can't you see how much more wonderful that is? Who wants to die in a room? Who wants to enter death *presumably*? Away with all that! When you really die you won't care whether you're buried or not, whether there be the tangible evidence of death or not. Death is for us, the living, and we'll see to it that you're properly buried. You see, when the sun shines and the larder is so easy to grasp. I don't want any tangible evidences. I don't need them. If the man is buried, well and good. If he is not buried, well and good too. Everything gets buried eventually. Time, time, it all takes a little time,that's all. It's so silly to worry about cemeteries and embalmers when the whole world is a cemetery and an embalming fluid. And it's so silly to wage an unholy battle for the preservation of one's precious ego when there is so little ego to go round.

13

What I am trying to say perhaps is that there is a real fight with the world which one wages perpetually and there is also a ghostly fight which one wages with oneself. The fight with the world is healthy, necessary and inevitable; the other produces no good, is entirely personal, and is in the nature of a disease. Where we part company time and again is this borderline; your diagnosis of the world condition is usually sound, but your own approach to the world, your acceptance of it as a human being, is faulty, or shall I say simply—unhealthy? There is a lack of synchronization between your sound and brilliant ideas and your way of living. This would not be so if what you call "truth" had really struck home. It would be impossible, once you had realized the truth, not to live your life in accordance with it. What you are living out now is the disease. It is this element of disease which makes it difficult for you to distinguish between the mask which you call the day face of the world and the mask which you don at will and call your other self. One is a natural mask, so to speak, grown involuntarily, a protective device like skin tissue; the other is dangerous, delusory and pathological. The lying, cultural mask which is the day face of the world may well be the antithesis of the real, the poetic, but the other dual self is the antithesis of the one, the indivisible, and has no validity except as the expression of a symptom. Whatever advance is made into the realm of art is at the expense of life; what makes the day face of the world so ugly to the individual, to the poet, that is, is the static, death-like quality of it. But this is a natural phenomenon which, as human beings ordained to a human rhythm, we are obliged to accept with more or less grace. In the daytime the poet goes to sleep, he snores, he farts now and then, or he wets the bed. The poet goes to sleep on the breadcrumbs of his cultural world. It's a lousy sight because everything that is crumbling inspires a certain horror as well as tenderness. But it's a real process, a real condition, and no power of man can eliminate it. It's as natural as evacuation. In fact, that's what it is. The poet evacuates the high place. He leaves a towering of shit behind him and in this monument of shit the people securely nestle themselves and make their life.

You pretend that all this might be avoided—or at least it might be destroyed. As a matter of fact, it is being destroyed over and over again,but what you fail to realize, it seems to me, is that it is being created again and again in the measure that it is destroyed. You warm up to the destructive aspect of your job but you refuse to recognize the creative aspects of it. You want to forget that you too are making your pile of shit. To you the smell is O.K. because it's *your* dung and not your neighbor's. But it's dung nevertheless—in the final aspect. Perhaps you are smiling already, rolling that word "necrophilia" over on your tongue. But you are mistaken if you think it is a love of dirt which inspires me. I simply want to recognize dung for dung and angels for angels. I can't pretend to myself that I see angels when I see dung, or vice versa. But I do know that they are co-existent and that the one produces the other. I am against confounding the two things, that is all.

When I criticize your way of living, therefore, I only mean to say that I detect a flaw in your attitude towards life. I see a confusion which arises out of a desire to amalgamate two thoroughly disparate elements of life. To be extreme I might even say these elements are what are called life and death. You want to glue them together, raise them to some intangible sphere where it is either all Life or all Death. You won't die or live; to you they are small letter words which have an ignoble ring. You don't like the antithesis, the natural conjunction and separation which they imply either singly or together. You want the body of life and the body of death but you won't take the trouble to grow so much as a finger in either direction. You want to go back to that state of equipoise which produced the body of Hamlet, to the eternal confrontation and nothing but the confrontation. On this hair-trigger line you want to walk the right rope to the tune of a schizophrenic duet. No prelude, equaling y, and the rope guaranteed to last forever. Meanwhile, despite the dizzy height the dung piles up. Meanwhile the angels are fluttering overhead. Meanwhile the earth turns round on its axis and the sun completes its orbit. Night and day, but you are neither asleep nor awake; you are dancing through the schizophrenic trance, the long twilight sleep in the astral blue. You neither take on flesh nor do you lose flesh. You are a constant, like God, like the weather, like the tides. You're an imperishable weathercock, variable and true as the weather itself, variable and true as God Almighty, variable and true as the tides. You are the fourth dimension itself, but that means that you are unseizable, untenable, unpredictable. You are an idea that somebody concocted, an idea grown out of the human psyche, inviolate, imperishable, but nothing more than an idea. If you want to affect us, if you want to nourish us, if you want to kill us off even, you will have to perish, as idea. You will have to create an idea of yourself which is something more or less than idea. You will have to throw a shadow which we can walk in, a shadow by which we can gauge your proximity, your very existence.

To throw this shadow you have to face the sun. You have to admit that the earth turns around on its axis once every twenty-four hours and that one day in the endless revolutions you will no longer be of this earth or of the sun but of all time. Or, you can turn your face away from the sun, hide away in a cave, and pretend that you are already dead, which is to say that you died spiritually. But this sort of dying fools nobody but yourself and it is always possible that you can be jerked back to life again. You simply enter a cataleptic state, like one of the sacred beetles in the tombs of the Pharaohs. You become a dormant microbe, waiting ten thousand or twenty thousand years for the moment to usher in the disease.

Suddenly your whole life seems like a grand eclipse; the sun was blacked out and you had never imagined there was a sun but only this black spot in front of the eyes, only you yourself and your idea of life. Then suddenly the cataract is removed, suddenly you see! And like the young man by the ocean shore you go hermantile. The labor of putting two and two together you leave to the blind. In one moment of time everything is hurtled into whack—like that! Henceforth no one has the power to disorganize your vision. They can kill you, they can break your body into bits, but the vision is inviolate. It simply is. When a man gets this sight havoc seizes the world. The philosophers and the historians may say that the time is not ripe—the time is never ripe for the historians and philosophers, except in the past—but the man who suddenly sees announces the time and the time is always ripe because it is one with his vision. To break this man, to destroy this vision, requires centuries and centuries of future time. And even then the vision is never completely destroyed, merely dimmed. Another man arises and it is the same vision. No time for writing books, no time for building philosophies. The man simply says that he sees and goes straight to his death. He walks seeing and saying, each step he makes, each word he utters a clear, clean break with the past. He has no memory, no hopes, no regrets. Neither has he wife or friends. Nor has he loyalty. He moves straight on with ice-cold compassion, the supreme master of irony, the chief actor in the drama of man.

When we attempt to describe the pattern of such a life we create a spiderweb in which we are strangled. Every attempt to discover a pattern is a spiderweb. In this web we may act with frenzy or lie still—it is all one. Man was born not to create a pattern but to fulfill himself. In fulfillment the memory is lost, the image wiped out; neither is there will since will implies a goal outside the self.

There where the road divides stands King Hamlet, skull in hand and the rapier between his legs. When we join forces with Hamlet all will be gravy again: we will recover the sacred body, the fountain of life, the interstitial glands. Hamlet will be standing there on the road waiting for us and when we catch up with him, fourth-dimensionally speaking, presto! Some one will touch a button and we shall all be back in the womb again squirming around like a sack of snakes. Well, it's a lovely picture and if it weren't that time presses I'd be inclined to join hands with you and take the long road back. But time presses! What lies ahead, unknown, draws me on.

14

July 15, 1936

I have just been out for a beer and a sandwich, at Zeyer's. Standing at the bar, looking out upon a deserted terrace, my mind goes back calmly and quietly to that night when we sat right here and projected the idea of this book. It seemed to me, reflecting on the genesis of the book, that whatever we have accomplished thus far must differ vastly from what any of us had imagined that night. And it seems to me now, casting a calm, quiet glance backwards and forwards, that that is what is always happening in life—this creative compromise between the imaginative and the actual. And it is just this compromise which finally one learns to appreciate, to accept as the thing-in-itself.

This is Hamlet, and not that which we dreamed it to be. Did something intervene? Did something mar the clear thought? We know that something did intervene, did mar, did diminish. That something is life, as this is life and as the embryonic too is life. In one of your very last letters, where you talk of the *contre-temps* men, I notice that you struggle again to express something which either I understand perfectly, in my own language, or else am absolutely deaf to. I notice that you speak of these men as those who are seeking to "liquidate the past and the present." They are, of course, the creative spirits and naturally they are against the age, out of joint with the times. but the trek back—that I don't understand. For the process of liquidation, as far as I can make out, represents a forward march and not a trek back. And here I want to revive the core of the subject as it now seems to reveal itself to me . . .

Somewhere recently you gibe at me for shouting at you: "Hamlet is within you!" since the disease which is the body of this book is that Hamlet within you you jeer at me for being obtuse. But it is just here that the question of "liquidation" arises. Somehow you have identified your personal problems with the world's problems. Tonight Jean Cocteau is sitting somewhere in the Far East writing his little reportage for *Paris-Soir*. Last night he was in Malacca and I took the trouble to read when he had to say about that strange world. It will not strike you as at all strange to hear that one of the things which impressed him profoundly last night was the thought of the utter unimportance of such a city as Paris. It had dwindled away, in the perspective of a true Frenchman's eye, to a mere microcosm. Sitting in Malacca. What impelled Jean Cocteau to move his precious skin and bones to that utterly strange, fantastic world of the East? *Money*, the average man will say. Money, yes . . . but that isn't all. Nor would the need of money account for the manner of this report, for the peculiar disquietude and nostalgia which emanates his writing. Cocteau, as you know, is a man not without a sense of destiny. Into everything he writes there enters a strong cosmic distillation, a very distinct, personal cosmic anxiety, if I may call it so, which is almost as strong as punk. I am thinking of Cocteau moving his precious skin and bones around, fulfilling his destiny. A year ago the thought of a trip around the world might have been utterly repellent, utterly unimaginable to him. Tonight he is sitting in the Far East and the little world which is so dear to him has dwindled to almost infinitesimal proportions.

What am I driving at? I am thinking of you, of your peregrinations, of myself and my own peregrinations, of so many of us, all moving about from her to there, *shuffled about*, is really the way it would seem. As we mere puppets? I don't think so for one moment. We are moving about in response to urgent needs, driven by secret inner forces, desires, impulses, hungers, of which we have only the barest inkling from time to time. Men have been moving about this way since time began—space-binders and time-binders. A restless energy, and endless quest, desires unfathomable. As we move about we curse the spirit that drives us on. We try to blame the world, the condition of the times, anything and everything we would attribute it to but our own selves. What are we trying to do, moving about thus? Well, for one thing, we are trying to "liquidate." We are trying to get rid of the past, our own personal past—*and* the present too, because the struggle to eliminate the past renders the present null and void. When you sit at the machine and write about the past that is in you you are not struggling any more, but moving, and you have a sense of time and that time is eternal and of the present. The Hamlet that you are today is a vastly different Hamlet than he was yesterday before you began to write about him, or should be, if you are honest with yourself. Personally I don't think you are honest with yourself, though I know you mean to be and do your best to be. But you are nursing Hamlet and coddling him, rather than liquidating him. If you had really wanted to liquidate you wouldn't have needed to write a line. You would have liquidated.

There is a sentence towards the close of this theme about the *contre-temps* men which concludes thus: "so that as far as I personally am concerned he (Hamlet) represents a mode of *artistic* self-liberation." You put *artist* in italics. What am I to infer from this? That your liberation as artist is an entirely different thing from your own individual liberation? Your aim, you add immediately, is to get a sense of life. Do you think that is accomplished *technically*, by an artistic device? Do you think you can be dead as man, as individual, and be alive as artist? Let me attempt to put things simply . . . When we speak of liquidating the past, our own personal past, what do we mean, generally speaking? Do we not mean ridding ourselves of the fears and obsessions which restrict our free expansion and make of the pattern of our lives a treadmill? Why do we wish so ardently to cut loose from the past? Because we feel bound to things which are no longer alive to us, which no longer have meaning for us. We want to get rid of the ghosts that stalk us. You say, we want to get back to "an earlier beginning in the spirit." But my dear fellow, there is no getting back to anything. There is only progression, or else lack of progression, which is dry rot, living death, the halt on the edge, as you put it. The men whom you characterize as against the times, are these men truly against the times—or is that not rather a way of speaking? Are they not more truly *of* the times? Why should we mince words? It is not possible for a man to be a great creative spirit and be *behind* the times—the idea is perfectly senseless and absurd. All these men are highly evolved types and the dislocation only serves to emphasize the fact. This is a fact which is as patent and as true now as it was during the Golden Age of Greece. When you confuse, or identify, the world problem with your own personal problem as artist, or as individual, you simply evince a lack of self-understanding, a lack of self-confidence. You are slated for an unhappy life, a discordant life—it's written in the stars. But a richer life than is accorded to those about you. Sometimes it is possible to have both—a richer life and a happier life, but that happens very seldom. That requires not only the utmost genius, but luck too, which may be described in terms of heredity, or in astrologic terms, it makes no difference. Some have it and some haven't. Most of us haven't. For most of us it must suffice to be able to have a richer life, and not merely to be in step with the world.

I was thinking of the peregrinations, the voyages, a little while ago. Because the essence of destiny seems to be in that idea of voyaging. And again the question comes up—*what kind of voyage?* From the time we open our eyes until we close them again it is a voyage. Most men spend their lives trying to blind themselves to the fact that they are taking a voyage. They are talking about the seasons and the toll of the seasons, but about what makes seasons and how to avoid them. It's very much like a man walking through a museum in which are gathered the world's masterpieces and saying to himself—"at five o'clock they will close . . . at five o'clock they will close." By five o'clock he will have seen only a small portion of the world's masterpieces and seen them, mind you, with a five o'clock eye. At six o'clock he will be on a train bound for another city and his mind, instead of being filled with masterpieces will be filled with regret that the museum closed so early. It rarely occurs to such a one to postpone the trip which he has planned and stay over. It suits him better to complain about early closings, or about the bad lighting, or this or that. To me, in my best, my clearest moments, the world is a marvelous museum filled with masterpieces. And in these moments I have the good sense to stay over and not take the next train out. I have also the good sense to forget what the critics have said about this picture and that and to realize very distinctly that the creation of the masterpieces, imperfect though they may be, was one thing and the opinions of the critics quite another. It is only when I am in no hurry to go anywhere that I can forget and enjoy, and that means living in the present, I take it. That means that the past is liquidated, my own past and the world's past too. Because in those moments I am not standing before a date and place but before all time, from the beginning to the end, and there is no more time because it is all time.

Look . . . you're taking a voyage, a unique voyage, and the only one you will ever take. Critically speaking, there are lots of things to complain about. But the voyage, don't forget that. Critical or uncritical, you will have to make it. You can, of course, at any time you choose, jump through the porthole. That's within every man's prerogative. But as your voyage you will discover that the best results are obtained by not squinting. Either close your eyes and dream it away, or open them wide and take in the landscape, the drama, the spectacle. Your father had a different voyage. Your grandfather had still a different voyage. Your son will have a different voyage too. Ulysses and Oedipus, they had grand voyages. So much so that we can't rid our minds of the thought. They were important voyages to us because we, in our frailty, accredited to them, to their voyaging, a quality of destiny which we deny to ourselves. Cocteau is voyaging now tonight. Less grand, but still a little of the flavor of destiny in it. He is voyaging to make money, to fill his empty pockets. That, perhaps, is what he says to himself. Meanwhile a fatal alteration is going on. Cocteau will come back with or without money, but not the same Cocteau. He may dream of going back to an earlier beginning, but there is no going back. He is going forward stained in Chinese ink. We are all going forward, some of us faster than others, that is all. None of us are going back, except in the mind, which is a delusion and an illusion. Some of us have liquidated the past, most of us will never liquidate the past. And finally, it is not the past which matters at all, because when we come into the full present the past is there and the future too and neither of them are frightening or bewildering. In the full present which is the living moment, we join forces with past and future. In that moment

Hamlet has no more importance than the *Minotaure* on my table, or the ash tray beside it, or the ashes in the ash tray. We forget and enjoy, and remember everything.

15

With every scrap of paper that goes into the waste basket upon the task it's really quite marvelous the satisfaction͏ you goes a thousand memories and associations. Once you embark derive from it. It helps to liquidate the past, "to abreact," as Rank would say, "the trauma of birth." That too is going into the waste basket in a day or two—I mean *The Trauma of Birth* I was rereading portions of it last night—to reassure myself that I had missed nothing by neglecting this ponderous tome, for I had only sniffed at it here and there in the past. I am convinced now that it means nothing to me. I see it now as a grand farrago, a potpourri of ideological pish-posh. Any theory that a Hottentot might erect on the subject would have an equal, if not a superior, value for me. I see nothing but the ferocious masturbative mechanism of induction and deduction at work. I see no grand truths! I laugh at the naive "explanations." This is a mania—*explaining* things. It goes with a certain type of mind which I abhor. And always leaves me with the feeling that nothing is explained, that we are simply eating into a hole. By contrast Lao-Tse on the *negative* aspect of things seems a thoroughly positive and contributory thought. I was sitting on the Boulevard Jourdan last night, over a book, musing on the importance of the unimportant. Anais was saying to me that when she was in good form a music seemed to emanate from all things, with each object a different rhythm, a different timbre, a different vibration. With me it has always been a music for the eye, a tremendous discord, disequilibrium, which throws into powerful relief the thoroughly insignificant, whether in a person or in a thing. At such moments I am in ecstasy because the disorder which confronts me is the most intimate order, the unique order which is being suppressed in me every day through mere necessity of living. The more insane the world appears the more liberated I feel. The feeling arises that nobody will ever be able to categorize this which passes through my mind. This is the essence of the poetic because it is susceptible of the utmost variety of transformation through the slightest pressure. It approaches the condition of music because it is fluid and unseizable, having the highest significance (for the one who experiences it) but absolutely impervious to "explanation."

Boulevard Jourdan . . . musing . . . the importance of the unimportant . . . A month hence, I may be sitting on Fifth Avenue, if I am, I am sure that I will not be musing. Somehow I can't believe that I will be sitting there. I can see myself sitting on a street in San Francisco, or in New Orleans, but not New York. And yet that is where I shall probably sit. That is, the ghost of me will sit there. The real me will be in China, or Darjeeling, or Timbuctoo. Timbuctoo! That reminds me of another fragment of last night. Could not one be just as happy in Timbuctoo? Why should France, or if you like, Spain, be the only place to live in? Speaking of France and for myself I can only say that here, in the highest measure that I have ever known, there seems to be a blending between inner and outer. Whatever the individual Frenchman created and thus made part of the environment, made impersonal, as it were, accords me the utmost freedom and harmony. If I cannot have an anarchic condition, where there would be no culture then I prefer the utmost culture. I believe that my own thought is very close to this—that at the point of highest civilization, at the moment of disintegration, the civilized man and the savage meet. It is at this point, as I keep repeating, this historical moment when a complete break is always imminent, always possible, that the miraculous lies in waiting, and this apprehension of the miraculous, this conviction of the power and the beauty of complete anarchy, is voiced by the dominant poets . . . your *contre-temps* men, in other words. What invalidates the social revolutionaries for me is the emphasis laid upon adaptation to environment. What invalidates the psychoanalyst for me is the stress upon adaptation—to one's own nature. Behind the idea of adaptation is the idea of failure. Neither the social environment, nor one's own nature is a valid norm. The norm is the abnormal! The earth, for example, is she adapting herself wisely to the celestial environment? Even the most sanguine philosophers cannot but admit that the end will be catastrophic. This even the physicists write in the margin of their cunning calculations and predictions. In raising himself above the animal state—by means of "symbol formation' ' "—the best that man succeeds in doing (and it's a poor best!) is to make the world over into a replica of his unconscious. Since the Unconscious is a residuum or a reservoir of repressed living the net gain is exactly nil, according to my calculations. It means further, as I see it, that contrary to the general impression, the image of the world which we call reality is simply the reflection of our criminal instincts. We have a criminal world without benefit of crime. That is, we have art, or the "arts," the excretory baggage, in other words, of the non-extirpated criminal in our midst. That is, we have a ghostly, fictive world which does not even satisfy the artist, who is the criminal at large. We have, in short, the triumphant satisfaction of living in the negative, as a reward for transcending the animal state. To make this negative condition more comfortable we have wholesale slaughter now and then, which restores the itch for more negation. Instead of "autoplasm" we have "alloplasm." This is "the essentially *human* primal phenomenon which enables human beings to become different from animals . . ." You can see why I have no further need of this book!

16

In a recent review of my *Tropic of Cancer* by a Frenchman I see that mention is made a number of times of the "homo Millerianus," i.e. a megalopolitan man of the Alexandrian stripe. This man is of the non-heroic type. Not quite the rock-bottom man of China, for the ashes have yet to be shaken down. If nothing more, he is, however, a man who has learned the wisdom of "satisfying his needs." These needs though largely and justly biological, are not exclusively so. In his leisure moments he reveals the cormorant's appetite for "the better things of life."

I mention these random phrases to emphasize this business of "satisfying one's needs." This phrase has become rather hollow only, as I see it, because men understand less and less as time goes on what constitutes their needs. You would be inclined to say, *if I understand you aright*, that their needs are purely biological—and hence unsatisfactory. But I am becoming more and more convinced that even when they talk of nothing but these basic biological needs they are nevertheless concerned with needs of a wholly different order. I am sorry to say, that as a race, I don't believe men have ever given enough heed to these purely physical needs. The struggle for bread, it seems to me has been rather the struggle for the communion loaf—*and hence* eternally unsatisfactory. Bread is always confused with justice, or with right, or with God, or with country. To eat is not to conjugate the Verb. These are two separate activities which if performed simultaneously bring about the direst confusion that a Mickey Mouse universe is born, for what is a Mickey Mouse

Universe if not the nightmare of indigestion? Here the stifled past asserts itself with a vengeance; it is not the realm of fantasy or reverie or dream which is born of a full stomach and a full activity. It is the realm of frustration created by trying to eat one's bread and conjugate the Verb at the same time.

As I go on in life I observe that there is less and less singing and more and more wailing. Or, I could also say that there is more and more argument and less and less truth. Or, I could go still further and say that there are more and more circles but less and less centers. You might object logically that there can be no circles without a center, and yet, like the stone which drops to the bottom of the lake and is lost, so we who stand upon the shore often to see the peripheral movement of the water without understanding the cause of that movement. The evidence of things unseen is there, but the power to believe is gone. For that one has to be able to accept the truth in the lower regions, to absorb it not ratiocinatively, but diaphragmatically. The step from perception to realization can be made in the twinkling of an eye, or it can take centuries. It depends on one's state of grace, which has nothing to do with acumen or logic, but with health. Psychological health. Men writing about truth are usually diseased; man talking about truth are likewise usually diseased. But men *acting* upon truth are usually sound and healthy. These men do very little talking or writing—*they sing*. This singing, and not the hairsplitting, gives us the impression of their very-much-aliveness. Also of emptiness in the sense that we are unaware of drag or slag, which to use more abstract terms we might call sorrow and memory.

And this reminds me of our friend Hamlet who, should I admit for the moment to be (a) of heroic stuff, most certainly was at no time the gay and negligent old rogue which the men of certitude were. Hamlet never sang, and when he laughed it was on the wrong side of the face. He had his counterpart in other times, among the confused and sour geniuses of Athens, Rome, Tyre, Babylon, Alexandria, Carthage, etc. In all times we have had men who were wrestling with ghosts and men who were too busy living to be plagued by such fears. The clever ones have been able to explain the presence of ghosts by this or that lingo, sometimes metaphysically, sometimes historically, sometimes economically, but the guys who had truth in their bowels never reckoned in ghosts or dialectics. They believed in God, so to speak, and they kept their bowels wide open. Catharsis was as natural as breathing and did not require the performance of an "Oedipus Rex."

And so, though I understand better why you wish to travel back along the radii to the center, I cannot understand why you wish to adopt a companion such as Hamlet who was a rueful, melancholy and confused spirit. If you have need of a companion at all I would rather nominate for you that unconscionable old scallywag Lao-Tse who would never have written a line had the Emperor not caught him by the tail and commanded him to do so. Lao-Tse apparently was quite able to get along without committing himself to paper; it was the Emperor and his vassals who had need of seeing the truth in words. And though I am grateful, in a way, to the Emperor for having obliged Lao-Tse to leave us a few cherished morsels of wisdom still I feel that had they not been put down we would have arrived there just the same. For I am convinced, as I say over and over again, that our problems are individual problems and that the times are permanently out of joint, look where you will. And so again I deplore the futile labor which is spent in realigning the external pattern. This external pattern is but the composite of the inner chaos and has not to do with man and society, but with man and man. It was no better in Shakespeare's day than today. In every age the men who were superior have been bullied and harassed, maligned, misunderstood, and usually gibbeted. This is but natural if you take things naturally. If, when Rome was the real center of the world, a cultured Roman could talk to another cultured Roman anywhere in that world with a high degree of understanding, so today can a cultured man of the world talk to another cultured man of the world with the same degree of understanding. You seem to forget, in your zeal to lay a theory, that these so-called "cultured" men have always been extremely rare and that in their private writings there has always been the same plaint, the plaint which you and others make, to wit, that the opportunities for genuine communication are so restricted. But the highest type of man usually arrives at a point beyond the need of the "cultured" man. He reaches a balance, an inner balance, which reconciles him to the world, or the world to him, as you like. He does that at the expense of the culture which produced him. He becomes a thoroughly anarchic, timeless individual. He relates himself to God, which is equivalent to saying that he discovers the Holy Ghost within him. This condition is not conducive to building up a society so-called. And a culture is dependent, *ipso facto*, upon a highly developed society.

The eternal soliloquizing of Hamlet is, like the eternal soliloquizing of our cultured individuals, only the expression of inner uneasiness, of unrest, of unfitness. The polarity which has broken down is not of necessity the loss of polarity between man and society but of the man and the self. To right the world is precisely the sort of futile, masochistic task which such men undertake because it is the surest guarantee against the duty of righting themselves. No religion, no government, no system of ethics can ever replace the voice of conscience which is man's infallible guide. Ideals fail because it is something imposed from without, because it is an effort to establish a theoretical totality. There is no totality possible in which we may all swim comfortably. There is for each and every one an integral totality limited by his own efforts. It is not ideal, abstract, flawless or permanent; rather it is tangible, immediate, flexible, quotidian. It is part of the sense of permanent joy which, in my opinion, is the only reasonable goal of life.

17

I would have grown up to be like every other American Jew- hater had it not been for the fact that I was a bit of a queer egg myself. I discovered soon enough another fact about myself—that I was different not only from the Jews about me but from the other Gentiles. In fact the difference between me and the other Gentiles was more threatening than the difference between me and the Jews, so it seemed at the time. And so, out of pure strategy, I suppose, I began to make allies of my Jew acquaintances. I began, in short, to *cultivate* them. It is to them I owe my initiation into the arts. The whole cultural pattern came to me via the Jews, as happens in many places throughout the world, wherever the soil itself is sterile or the people "backward," as we say. During this period I was an ardent champion of the Jew. I practically walked out on my Gentile friends in favor of the sensual seductiveness which the Jews offered me. Strange now to say that, for today I no longer can see the Jews in this light. It is precisely the sensual element which I find woefully lacking in them. But in America, by comparison with the Puritan sterility, they were sensuous and sensual. If I had never come to Europe and experienced a culture at first hand I would still be muddled on the subject. My life amidst the French has opened my eyes to the meaning of culture. And so, whenever we get to discussing that "lying cultural mask" I make a little reservation about your discernment because the very word "mask" conveys to you a different content from what it conveys to a Frenchman or a German or a Pole, or what you like.

With regard to the mask one always feels that the Jew is somewhat like the magician at the circus. One feels that he has been clapping the mask on and flinging it off so often that he has lost all respect for the mask. He uses it as part of his act, so to speak. Now, of course, this is not the meaning of the mask, neither in the Nietzschean sense nor in the old Roman sense of *persona*. The mask, in the deepest sense, is something which, if it were stripped off, would reveal not the naked reality, not the real face of the individual, but the mask's own impress. The mask would be found to be *real*, as in the celebrated tale of Max Beerbohm's. If this were not so a culture would have no meaning. The culture becomes the mold of the soul of the people—not a false face which can be thrown in the gutter when the carnival is over. What often creates uneasiness for a Gentile, when he is among Jews, is the sure instinct that the Jew has no such feeling about the mask. About the culture, that is. The very facility with which the Jew puts on the cultural mask is what alarms the Gentile. You speak in one of your recent letters of having lost the unity of your person, through the confrontation with New York. I think I understand that. Did not the same thing threaten me? Was I not split by my conflict with the whole American scene? In New York you are always minus, you write. You question whether you are real, whether you truly exist. Of course New York, America, threatens all unity of person everywhere. America is the schizophrenic Paradise—have I not made that clear to you yet? to go to America in any other guise but that of a traveler, a visitor, is disastrous. It would be senseless to think of adapting oneself to America: it would be like adapting yourself to the very disease you are fighting.

But what produces the conflict? Why the fact that the disease is still virulent in you. You say it is hopeless, you are too old, the world is too old. I don't see that at all. You are quite right in regarding the American thing as part of a larger problem, part of the historical problem: the death of a culture. (What Hamlet has to do with it all, incidentally, I don't know, since in the progression towards a definite end the Hamlet problem disappears with the others automatically. But your individual problem should be greater than the cultural problem, and not merely identified with it. Idealism may, as you wish it, be at the root of all cultural patterns, but it seems to me that the individual always precedes the culture. And it also seems to me that the human individual may one day rid himself of the tyranny of the ideal. It seems to me not only quite possible, but inevitable, that one day we human beings will live an entirely a-historical life. This very question of becoming one day truly a *human being* implies, for me at any rate, a state of existence in which the recidivist tendency, inherent in all our aborted idealistic striving, will vanish. History covers only a short span of human endeavor, human evolution. I am not at all sure that the cyclical aspect of our historical life will not give way one day to another, to a seemingly anarchic one in which we move not within definite cultural limits but within unlimited *human* ones based on the realization of our own potentialities.

Where there is Hamlet there is thinking, you say. Hamlet stands for culture and tradition. Well, if that be true then I am glad to know that Hamlet is disappearing.

On the one hand, you see, you want to see Hamlet liquidated; and on the other hand you want to preserve what Hamlet stands for. The real self, which you are continually denying, want to deal the death blow to Hamlet; but that other self, which is identified with the historical process, doesn't want to see Hamlet polished off because it *is* Hamlet. The ability to think which you say is of the essence of Hamlet is the very thing which ruined Hamlet, which destroyed the unity of his person. Because Hamlet somehow is identified in our minds with the wrong kind of thinking, with thinking, let us say, raised to the nth degree. I have no fear of man losing his power to think: it is simply impossible. Man will think and feel and act, as long as he is man. But, as in an end period like ours, thinking can dominate feeling and acting—and that is the only significance Hamlet in my mind. The fact that he is out of control. In this sense Hamlet *is* mad, and I agree with the louts who do not understand the significance of the drama. (Try to imagine here that *Hamlet* would sound like to the Chinese!) Of course I understand quite well your objection to the New York interpretation of the play. Here the typical American love of the sensational comes into play. Nothing is understood there except as pathological phenomenon. A *mad* Hamlet is exciting drama; a noble Hamlet staging a sound conflict would be incomprehensible to them. Now I am not immune to the dramatic value of soul conflicts, only I would say—Hamlet's soul conflict leaves me cold. Frankly, I don't know what it's all about. What interests me a great deal more than the Hamlet problem, as Shakespeare gave it to us, is the attitude of Shakespeare himself, as revealed by the changes he made in the official version of the play. There, it seems to me, is a drama worth studying, a drama which antedates Hamlet and which supersedes it also. This is the drama which I see you playing out also, in your own way. This is the drama which occurs through dividedness. This is, if you like, the drama of the Jewish people. I mean by that, trying to serve God and Mammon at the same time. The great tragedy which befell the Jews came about through their failure to recognize the living God. You know very well, when I say a thing like this, that I am not talking like that crazy pastor whom you met on the boat, who went out to Poland to save a few miserable souls. I have no more interest in Christianity than I have in Hamlet, I hope that's clear. But I do see one thing clearly, that the Jews have kept alive the idea of an Absolute, and in doing so they have made themselves cursed. It is this same shadow of the Absolute which made Hamlet such a hopeless wreck. Liquidate Hamlet and you liquidate the pernicious notion of the Absolute.

To give you a little better idea of what I mean let me tell you about my friend Hans Reichel who was just here a moment ago. Hans Reichel is a painter, a poetic, mystical painter of the old German school. Twice a week I go to him for instruction in the technique of making watercolors. Whether I ever learn to make a good water color is really unimportant. In going to Hans Reichel twice a week I get something far more valuable than mere instruction in the use of a technique. Every time I see Hans Reichel I feel a little more holy. Yes, *holy*. I think if I were to say to Reichel one day: Reichel, what do you think about the Absolute?—he would look at me in utter amazement. I don't think the word means anything to him. And yet Reichel is living a sort of Absolute life of painting. Punctured, it is true, by occasional sprees in which he breaks a rib or adds a new scar to his already well-scarred face. Hans Reichel lives by God's mercy. He has absolutely no hopes of earning a living, but he goes on painting every day just as though he were being subsidized by a Maecenas. Every day of his life Hans Reichel paints a fragment of the living universe. The question of the whole, of the meaning of the universe, never enters his head. But the meaning of the whole is there in every picture he makes, no matter even if it be the size of a pinhead, his painting. He is always feeling and acting, and what thinking he does is related to his feeling and acting, as regards his paintings. If he reads a book it can just as well be "Mile High" as Plato's "Republic." In fact, he would enjoy the former much more. He admits it. I know many men like Reichel who, when they put aside their work for the day, can seek amusement, recreation and instruction, or renewal, in simple, homely pursuits. Reichel, for instance, spends a good many evenings with the Arabs who life in his quarter—in their bistrots, I mean. He finds it better than going to a movie, more stimulating, more refreshing. They are not intelligent Arabs; they are just plain workmen who like to drink and gamble and fight after hours. They are silently and unwittingly collaborating with Reichel in the production of his pictures.

Now what I mean to say by all this is that in the presence of Reichel one feels the eternality of things. Everything is simple, because life itself is simple to him. He is living with us in our time under the same conditions, and living with far less hope of reward than any of us, but I do not hear him complain (I hear him say from time to time very urgently: "Miller tomorrow I must have a few francs!" and that is all). How is it then that he is not in despair? How is it that he is able to go on painting every day just as if he were doing God's own bidding? How is it that he can take his daily walk through the Parc Montsouris and look at the birds and the fish and wonder about them? And when he talks to me about the birds and the fish I begin to laugh and weep. This man is really in communication with life and you know it the minute he opens his mouth. You know he is in communication with God when he invites you to sit down at the table with him and study the watercolor. His whole manner is one of utter simplicity. He needs only a sheet of paper, a little pot of water, his brushes and paints. He never makes a generalization. He says, sitting before the blank piece of paper— "now just supposing, Miller, that you are taking a walk with me through the street. Let us say it is just about this time, the moon is already out, and everything is getting very quiet. I am sure Miller, that what you see now is different from what you would see any other time of the day..." And so on. Before very long we are standing inside the house which we are making together on the little sheet of paper. There is a bathroom which he has laid out very thoughtfully for me (and even a bidet, too), there is also a studio with plenty of light (he couldn't forget the windows), and a sleeping chamber, and so on. Also the stairs. Naturally there must be stairs to climb up to the apartment from the street. And there must also be a door downstairs. It goes on like that, very simple, from one thing to another. Always in life and always a moon or stars or a little flowerpot or fishes in the pond. We don't talk about God, nor duty, nor the ghost, nor Communism, nor aestheticism. We talk sometimes about the good wines of France, about the creaking table loaded with things to eat, about the color of a partition wall in some ruined house down the street. The pattern left on the old wall reminds Reichel of the life led by the former inmates of that house. It doesn't remind him of the historical cycle, or of astrophysical theories. It reminds him—the faded blue wallpaper, for example— of the crazy *bonne* who lived in the attic. But just the same, he is grateful to that crazy *bonne* for having left that beautiful patch of blue on the charred wall. He sees the mark of the stairway and he thinks of how she ran up and down the whole day long waiting on the selfish mistress. He thinks of the little mirror she hung up over the washstand and of how she looked at herself every day and perhaps thought she was beautiful. He goes like that, from zone to zone, quietly picking daisies, as it were. To me it's a cure: it teaches me something about living. And when I leave him, usually in bright moonlight, for the moon has been coming out bright and clear recently, I always think how wonderful it is to be alive, just to see things just to hear and taste and smell. The simplest things seem quietly miraculous to me and I feel that everything is right and in its place. And I know then that if it is not so the fault is with us.

The word *liquidating* which crops up again and again in your letters—do you know what I think of when I encounter it in your letters? I think of the mind chopping itself into raw spinach. I know in my heart and soul that you are liquidating nothing: you are not even liquidating your own saliva. You say, apropos of Western culture, that we should not kill it *within*. There are two words in this sentence which destroy the meaning of your thought: *should* and *within*. The "within" relates to what I said a while back about the mask and the attitude of the Jew towards the mask. That part of you which belongs to the New York complex is what keeps alive something "within" which is already dead. If the culture is really dead—and I thoroughly believe it is—then it is because it died first "within." And you know that very well with your head, because when you talk of Karl Marx and the application of his theories to a pooped-out world you hit it on the head. The thing is, you are not patient, you are not easy in your own soul. Let time work its leaven. Accept time absolutely, with Walt and all the other brave souls. That's what it means "to render unto God what is God's and unto Caesar what is Caesar's." But I notice that when you begin to render unto Caesar you are profoundly disturbed; you feel guilty before God. Now I can tell you, my dear Fraenkel, that God is not in the least worried about such things. He knows that you have to make a living, and if you'd only trust Him implicitly I'm sure he'd see you through. This morning I awoke, very much refreshed after a twelve hour sleep, and I had much the same feeling. I said to my bedmate: "One day I shall go to bed with my notes spread out on the table for the next day's work and I shall die quietly and tranquilly in my sleep. And do you think I shall worry whether the book was finished or not? No, somebody else will take it up and carry on, that I know. And the notes will be filed away and the books will be carted to the library and everything will go on just as before—I shall die very tranquilly in my sleep and leave everything unfinished." And I can say a thing like that, let me tell you very honestly, because what is dead in me is dead and doesn't bother me any more. I saw last night at your recommendation "The Charge of the Light Brigade" and I came away very much disgusted with all such films and all such themes. I came away feeling absolutely convinced of my *depaysement*. I don't know what such charges are all about. All I could think of, during the celebrated charge, was of the real horses and the real men who took part in that scene, as to how many broken limbs and broken bones there were and as to how many horses had to be shot afterwards because all their hopes of trotting and charging hereafter had been rendered nugatory. (To render nugatory one's hopes—that's a little phrase came to my head from "The Magic Mountain." A beautiful little phrase which always makes me quite jolly. Any man who can coin a phrase like that has lost the meaning that underlies the phrase. And so I sit on the other side of the frontier, beyond good and evil, as it were, and I laugh at him and at his hopes rendered nugatory.) And here I must convey to you a little message concerning the film. We were discussing the stupidity of it and then, after all was said and done, I exclaimed "I suppose it was a good film!" This truck the other person as the apotheosis of doubt. And so I sent it along to you, with my good wishes, adding per corollary— from "doubt's duck with the vermouth lips."

All this relates to the world "should" which you use so frequently. Western culture is dead. Well, what's to do? Why not let it die a natural death? You see the problem which is torturing you is a purely personal one. You have made yourself Hamlet by splitting in two. And it's a jolly fine spectacle you put on, but understand me, it's purely private. What you are trying to liquidate is the unlived residue that makes up your memory. *Inasmuch as* or *in so far as*— take your choice, these are your own expressions— if you do not live out your own life you will be plagued by anterior and posterior problems: on the one hand Hamlet, on the other hand the historical problem. Some day you will find it in your own interest to just *be* Michael Fraenkel and take the full consequences for being such. You will grow a new body which will fit you like a glove, because it will be your own. And God will be the tailor. You can't have two tailors working for you at the same time. If he's a good tailor, and I personally can recommend God to you as an excellent tailor, you won't need to look elsewhere. Right now you're trotting about, going from one shop to another, and nothing is ever quite satisfactory. Nothing will ever be satisfactory, I can predict that in advance. Because the Mexican tailor, like the American or the French tailor, is not making the clothes to order. Sometimes it rains too much, sometimes there's too much sun. Sometimes they speak such strange languages that you can't understand what they as you. For instance, latterly they've probably been suggesting to you that they would include with your tuxedo a nice little gas mask which may be worn inconspicuously beneath the lapel of your coat. You go to another place and they will suggest undoubtedly a beautiful waistcoat of mail. And so on. Now my experience in these little matters, has been that, however a la mode these little changes may be, they are in the last resort ineffectual and fundamentally intolerable, uncomfortable, God doesn't make any of these new fandangled vestments. He doesn't go in for the latest fashions. He's thoroughly conservative. Usually he makes only miraculous clothes that carry you through with a whole skin. Not always, to be sure. He keeps his own ends in mind, always. And when He makes you a new suit it's better not to make too many inquiries. Just take it and charge it up. Of course you are apt to look a little ridiculous in the eyes of the fashionplate men and women. You may not be invited for the grand ball or for the fete at the Opera. On the other hand, because of the miraculous quality of God's garments, you are apt to find yourself in strange places, strange situations. You are apt to find things going along swimmingly, and yourself in the swim, as it were. When you write a poem, for example, you will certainly not be worried about missing buttons on your fly. For you won't have a fly, do you see. Nor even a zipper. And naturally there are never any moth-holes either. Everything is miraculously provided for—including the poem. If you have a little death on your hands—you reel it off unerringly and without effort. Absolutely without effort. Effort is never directed towards the poem, mind you, but towards the plaguy buttons that are missing or the rendezvous that you forgot to keep or the letter you meant to write or the liquidation you forgot to liquidate. Professor Thiberge understands it perfectly. That's why he can write without the slightest cheek—"the prodigy is the normal." Do you get me?

Now underlying this idea of the Tailor-Made Suit is the idea of a perfect automatism which clears the air of *should* and *ought* and *must* and *will*. If you struggle you are lost. You begin at the very beginning—with a metronome. The metronome is extremely important. Without it you will make no progress. For example, supposing as must frequently happen to you, you just can't tie your tie this morning. First of all, please forget all that you were taught about tying your tie. Because it was all wrong, what they taught you in school. (Even Plato said—"there is no *will* in my system, no place for it.") Don't try to tie your tie all at once. Just put one flap over the other . . . the very first step. Or perhaps we'd better go back still further and try the simple act of slipping it around the neck. Do that with the metronome, say twenty or thirty times, at a speed of 50 to the minute. As I say, don't try to tie your tie today! Be content with having slipped it around your neck twenty or thirty times at the speed of fifty to the minute. Tomorrow, if you can do it at that speed without making a slip, you may go on to the next phase of tying the tie, which is to put one flap over the other. You see, parenthetically, and you must admit, that even an idiot can be taught this much. And the more of an idiot you are the more you will enjoy it, *with the metronome*. Of course, you don't keep it at 50 to the minute. You speed it up a little more each day. When you can perform the simple act of slipping it around your neck at 120 to the minute without a single slip you have arrived. You need never worry about that step again. The instincts, the automation in you, what I mean to say, will take care of it forever afterwards. And please realize right here, that you have already made a great advance over the majority of men. Because there are men in this world who, though they have sufficient intelligence to explain the Einsteinian theories, cannot slip a tie around their necks without fussing and fuming. (And, if I may say so, had they first learned to tie a tie properly, they might not be bothering about Einsteinian theories. This too is fairly important. Or we might all be living in a world *without ties*. Still more important!)

I don't think it is necessary for me to continue with the example. Apply it to all phases of living, from washing your neck to playing a musical instrument, or to making love. The metronomic system of automatic perfection. In the process you will please observe that many of our so-called problems have dropped by the wayside. Where, for example, is our old friend Neurosis? Where is our old friend Communism, or Capitalism? Gone by the boards. Problems as such tend to disappear completely. There are, to be sure, new situations every day, but they are not met with the old mechanisms.

They are met with an intelligence that is free to function. They are solved individually.

I recall a phrase like this, from your last letter: "with the whole past tradition wiped out there will be some hope!" The wrong word again is *whole*. Also "wiped out." You see, we don't *wipe out* whole past traditions. It just ain't done. Nor should we even desire to do so. Traditions get killed off in one's sleep, so to speak. If you struggle to kill them off—either within or without—you only keep them alive that much longer. The best remedy is not the homeopathic one you recommend but a much simpler one. Take it into your system assimilate it, absorb it and pass it off as excrement. That's the way of all flesh and has always been recommended by such eminent physicians as Mencius, Hippocrates, Galen, et alia. The only way in which we may be permitted to concern ourselves about the "whole" of anything is with regards to meaning, significance. There you can go the whole hog. But there again, if you really catch the significance of anything you are beyond the point of it being a problem for you. Here intelligence really does count, because it *is* intelligence at work and not just *intellect*. By this token you are deficient in intelligence though astounding *qua* intellect. And of course you don't know what the hell I'm driving at and that's what makes it delightful to write you these long letters. Hamlet is as useful to me, to my purpose, as any other subject. If you want me to help you liquidate, very well, I will liquidate with you—but in my own way. I liquidate continually: that's how I keep solvent morally and spiritually. If we are at the end of the Hamlet tradition, every well, we are at the end. If Western culture is dead, fine, let it stay dead. If men do not think any more, in your fashion, good then they are thinking in another fashion. But at bottom I know nothing is ended, nothing is dead, and men have not stopped thinking. I believe in life's processes, whatever the hell that means. One thing I know very definitely it means—it means that there is no use opening another drug store, no use handing out pharmaceutical remedies. I have no recommendations to make, no prescriptions to hand out. Let the sick languish, let the diseased rot, let the dead die.

When I read Spengler and Lawrence I was intoxicated with this shadow of doom which threatened us. I think the diagnosis was excellent. I think the facts are being corroborated every day. But I know damned well now that I am not doomed! That part of me which belongs to the world, to the collective life, to culture and tradition, yes—it is doomed. But I have accepted that and so it's not a bugaboo. Nor is it a daily masochistic treat which I serve up for myself at breakfast, lunch and dinner. I am a human being and a living part of the cosmos. I may also be a man who belongs to a certain epoch, imbued with certain ideas born of that epoch. I may be a citizen of this or that country, speaking this or that language. But don't derive my sustenance by reason of these facts.

There will be a smashup soon, you say, and maybe I shan't have time to run to a bombproof cellar. Quite possible. Well, then I shall be killed. Naturally, with my sound instincts for self-preservation, I shall try to get out in time—and probably will. On the other hand, it may suit me to stay and run the risk. I leave these things for the proper moment. To run to cover now is idle. Who can guarantee a perfect cover? I may be run over by a bicycle trying to flee to Elsinore. My destiny, I feel, is in my own hands. The minute I entrust it to the railway companies, or to a neutral government, or to the wide spaces, I run into new dangers, new snags. The trouble with Oedipus was that he saw the whole. And one can't live with the whole. One has to live day by day—and that is the only kind of perfect whole one can make.

Similarly, when we began this book we were not to worry about the whole. Things were to take their natural, logical, inevitable course. The daily increment born of daily living. The day book of the day face problem. *Voila!* But every now and then I feel you pulling me by the bit. Whoa! you cry, we're not getting anywhere. But where were we to go? My friend, did we not make ourselves free first? This was to be the sheer delight of not getting anywhere, which of course is to get everywhere. I tell you, I never worry about this book or where it will lead to. I am just as solvent now as I was when I commenced.

18

September 7, 1937

It's something like this—"the impermeable and infundibular parts are mutually disproportionate." It is only as I fail to understand you that everything waxes clear. For the last two months I have had on my desk a few notes intended to help me write the next Hamlet letter. One of them, which I had hoped to be the inspiration for a long excursus, reads "blankness of mind." As all the notes were made during my reading of Chuang Tzy's philosophy I take it that this particular note referred to one of the refreshing Taist principles which, as you know, are the source and mainspring of my vitality.

To wit: "The true Sage ignores God. he ignores man. He ignores a beginning. He ignores matter. He moves in harmony with his generation and suffers not. He takes things as they come and is not overwhelmed. How are we to become like him?"

If there is ultimate antithesis to Western thinking, Western feeling, in Chinese philosophy then it comes to full expression in a little paragraph such as I have just given you. But it is an antithesis, let me quickly add, which is not only comprehensible to the Western mind, but also acceptable to it. There is no Chinese fence around such an utterance; once formulated it becomes the common property of *mankind*. Or, perhaps I should qualify by paraphrasing thus: "it becomes the common property of all those who are ready to receive it." What distinction there is between East and West lies only, so it seems to me, in a stubborn, willful blindness on the part of one to the other. For myself I can say, for example, that I have a great deal more in common with Lao-Tse than with Jesus Christ, or with

Mohammed. I might also add, and with justice, that I believe I have more in common with Lao-Tse than have the great majority of his countrymen now alive, or than the great majority of his countrymen had in times past. And by the same token I have very little in common with Shakespeare, or with Immanuel Kant, or with Plato or with Spinoza.

The Master Lieh Tzu said: "He who uses silence in lieu of speech rally does speak. He who for knowledge substitutes blankness of mind really does know."

And then, as though anticipating the Hamlet-Faust controversy which was to take shape some twenty centuries or more later, one of the great sages spoke thus to his disciple: "Investigation must not be limited, nor must it be unlimited. In this undefinedness there is no actuality. Time does not change it. It cannot suffer diminution. May we not, then, call it our great Guide? Why not bring our doubting hearts to investigation thereof? And then, using certainty to dispel doubt, revert to a state without doubt, in which doubt is doubly dead?" Now some men seem to be all certainty and yet they give off an effuvia of doubt. For they are certain only of what they have formulated in thought, in words, but of what is unformulated, unknown to them, they are not at all certain. These are the victims of cruelest doubt, the veritable "doubt's duck with vermilion lips" discovered by Isidore Ducasse.

Dostoievski understood it. Take his speech of Stavrogin's from "The Possessed": "From me nothing has come but negation with no greatness of soul, no face. Even negation has not come from me. Everything has always been petty and spiritless. Kirillov, in the greatness of his soul, could not compromise with an idea, and shot himself; but I see, of course, that he was great-souled because he had lost his reason. I can never lose my reason, and I can never believe in an idea to such a degree as he did. I cannot even be interested in an idea to such degree. I can never, never shoot myself. I know I ought to kill myself, to brush myself off the earth like a nasty insect; but I am afraid of suicide, *for I am afraid of showing greatness of soul.*"

Lately, reading the life of the great Buddha, I was impressed by the utter simplicity of his ways. As you know, when he had come to the realization of his great role he stripped himself of all worldly possessions, including his wife and child, and renouncing the world went forth with a begging bowl, secure in his own strength. When he died, at the ripe old age of 82 or 83, he was laid on a cloth of gold and from his naked body there radiated a mysterious bright aura which was his sanctity. He had tried to eliminate sorrow and suffering from life, which was a mistake, but the effort was so great, so effective, that his influence is still incalculable. Next to Lao-Tse I consider him the greatest figure that the world has seen.

What I am trying to emphasize, by all these allusions, is that in the case of every great soul the man presented a face to the world. You are only presenting your disgust, which is like saying—*your ass*. None of these men were understood immediately, except by a very few. If only *one* had understood it would have been sufficient to them. That is another point which it is important for you to grasp. But to get the faith of another one has also to believe in the other. Chesterton understood when he said—"Of St. Francis it is far truer to say that the secret of his success was his profound belief in other people." That is something you have never learned and that is why you can employ the most hairsplitting logic and never arrive anywhere, never convince anybody, never more anybody. You have first got to move from your own spot, a forward reach with hands outstretched and ready to embrace. You have got to show your effulgent face and not your backside. Only the lord is permitted to show his hinder parts, as he is reported to have done with Moses. And when you attain the sanctity of a Buddha you may show your whole body and it will glow and sparkle like a twenty-two carat gold ring.

I must explain, in passing, that I am rereading St. Augustine now, making annotations in the margin, because an English bookseller assures me that a book thus marked by my own hand will fetch five to six pounds. I find this an easier way to earn a little loose change than to sit down and write an essay or short story, which nobody accepts anyway. Annotating at a paid rate is a very pleasurable job. It doesn't matter much what I write in the margins, so long as it is in my own hand.

It is not at all strange to me, consequently, to find you complaining about unintelligibility. The blood of the old womb is still ringing in your ears. The umbilical cord is still tightly fastened about your neck. The two words are "commingled and commixed" as St. Augustine puts it. Your feet are in the void, your head is in the noose. Naturally you are talking about the world all the time, meaning thereby a transient and temporal condition. Between your lingo about "living out the tradition" and the revolutionary lingo about the "historical materialism" there is no ultimate difference. You are both trying to find a new body—*but without a soul*. There is a difference between you, to be sure, but it is only as concerns the point or time of fixation. The revolutionaries are caught in the imaginary wheel of a future state which will be more or less compatible with their desires, their hopes, their aspirations; you are caught in the imaginary wheel of the past, when and where, to your thinking, there was hope and desire and aspiration. They are moving clockwise and you are moving counterclockwise, but it is the clock that you both have your eyes on. This becomes more apparent in your case when you talk of abolishing the clock. It means that the clock is still functioning in you, that the clock is very real. Each event in your life, whether for good or for ill (and who can ever say which is which?), instead of carrying you forward along your ordained path serves to stop you dead in your tracks and make you look backward. It was exactly the same mechanism which we observe in Hamlet. If he moves at all, it is backward like the crab. Every little incident brings him to a dead halt, to analysis, to self-mortification. If the Hamlet problem had been in your blood, as you said when you commenced the book *(this book)*, instead of your head, each day of your life would only have served as a marvelous springboard to another chapter of the book. If the problem had been real the book would have been gloriously unreal, that is to say, reality itself. But since it is an unreal problem which you have created by avoiding your real problems the book becomes real, becomes Hamlet, that is. Which is what was to be eschewed, was it not? You probably think I am being casuistical, in saying this. I am not. I notice, in glancing back over your letters, how frequently you accuse me of going off the path. Where are we getting? you constantly ask. The very question implies a misunderstanding of our task, or rather, our pleasure. It is this direct, purposeful, pragmatic attitude (towards everything) which is the essence of the non-understanding mind. The great problem, which is to live, is lost in the welter of little problems about living. If one cannot give himself up to the joy and mystery of the big interrogation mark the little ones will certainly not compensate for the loss. One should abandon himself to a problem, not concentrate upon it.

In your letters it seems to me that you constantly strike a false attitude, a pose. You pretend to make Hamlet the grand problem, when you know in your heart and should that it is not. Each letter seems to close the issue instead of opening it. It is again, let me say, very similar to the tactics of the Marxians. We begin with the revolution and we end with the revolution: the revolution itself never comes off. You know, I am sure, that there will never be a revolution such as these lads are dreaming of. At the very best there will only be this dream of a revolution such as these lads are dreaming of. At the very best there will only be this dream of a revolution which they are now living through. Between living out such a dream and living out a nightmare there is very little difference, to my way of thinking. The revolution itself becomes unreal: it is the dream which becomes more and more real. And finally the reality of the dream too is punctured because in their unilateral scheme of life there is no antinomial dream and walking sort of existence. Now it is the same with you *vis a vis* the Hamlet problem. In an abstract, purely cerebral way, you admit of a non-Hamlet world, or way of life. You admit it, however, only because logic demands it. But this purely mental clarity which allows you to talk *about* the problem prevents you utterly from living the problem, or expressing it artistically. To Shakespeare it was a reality, about that I have no doubt whatever. For him it was a personal problem and one well lived out. That is why the significance of it still pervades us, or haunts us, rather. But you have taken it literally, instead of symbolically, and now it is in your wool and you can't shake yourself free of it. But it is not real with you, therefore. On the contrary. For you it is a very convenient piece of armor behind which to deploy your very real suffering, which is of another order entirely. You stand between the world of Hamlet and the world of non-Hamlets.

You probably noticed the other day in the newspaper that an eminent psychologist had predicted that, if the American people continue to become hopeless schizophrenics at the rate they now do, in a hundred years from now, or less, there will be more schizophrenics than normal people in that country. You will see at once, I am sure, that no such thing can possibly take place. This is an error which not only the psychologist is prone to make, but also the statistician, the historian, the sociologist and all other false prophets. For it must be as plain as the nose on one's face that as we approach that glorious condition imagined by the psychologist and the statistician the very notion of schizophrenia will have completely altered. We shall enjoy an entirely different mental climate in which the notion of schizophrenia will be happily absent. There is a false attitude towards the future, shared by pessimists and optimists alike, in which an absolute, the new or different, is posited. Buddha, St. Augustine, Christ, Mohammed, Lenin, Rousseau—all of them were imbued with this fallacious notion. And you, despite your boastful realistic stand, are in the same boat. You describe the condition of affairs with remarkable accuracy, but your predictions are unwarranted because they ignore the constancy of the human psyche. In theory you can bring the world to a halt and examine it under the glass; actually there is no stop possible, and even your analysis, however timely a diagnosis it may appear to be, must be off by a considerable margin. The worst aspect of a lifetime pursuit such as yours is this, that in playing the doctor to the world you ignore your own illness. The others are suffering as you are suffering—for the very same reasons. It is a hopeless game of catch as catch can. Every one sees the other as a victim, or patient; a colossal imaginary picture of disease is built up which nobody can cure. The first step is to abandon the therapeutic role entirely. The next step is to give yourself up fully to the illness. The third step is to die, and the next is to be resurrected—*into the same world and the same conditions*, but with a new orientation. When you accept the world as is you alter it profoundly, because you have first altered yourself. Even the dullest-minded Communist is aware that the real secret of futility lies in the unwillingness, or unreadiness, of the individual to assume the full burden of responsibility. Even Communism must be inaugurated *by men*, by individual Communists. To my way of thinking the men who have actually been anything fully, unreservedly, wholeheartedly have been very few, a mere handful. The man who writes a book about anything, about something, that is, which he desirous to see brought about, is not that thing himself. The moment he has it, or is it, he is silent—he becomes the thing completely and reveals it through action in every moment of his walking life. The rightness or wrongness of a belief matters little in the face of a passionate, active belief. Even enthusiasm disappears, because enthusiasm is already a sign of not quite possessing it. Neither is one happy, in the ordinary sense, because having it, one is beyond happiness just as he is beyond sorrow. No matter by what label, what it is called, once a man has IT the face of the world is altered. One man can do it—with IT. It has been done time and again.

The fact that we retain a memory of the dead and departed has nothing to do with not accepting death. It comes to this, that what the ordinary jackass can do with ease you cannot do. You have made a fetish of death out of fear of it. When you run on the talk of Hamlet's attitude towards death you give it your own peculiar interpretation and call it Western. Of course Hamlet isn't interested in knowing the "secret" of death; Hamlet is *obsessed* by the fear of death. Hamlet is death and Hamlet sows death everywhere, just as you do with every line you rite and every word you utter. Hamlet is, as you say, "interested in life," but as a man who is interested in something beyond his grasp. You show the same curious avidity for life. Anybody who is interested in the secret of a thing is obsessed by that thing and thereby puts it beyond his grasp. The man who is in life and alive is not interested in the secret of life. A man who is interested in the secret of life is already dead. Of course it is easier for us to believe we are immortal; men have had this belief for thousands of years. They will continue to have this belief for thousands of years to come. There is nothing strange about it, nor is there anything strange about their holding the notion of mortality at the same time. The duality of man's nature is an ineluctable factor of human consciousness; it is only the thinker who is absurd enough to try to argue it away. One can know and accept the reality of death without pretending at the same time to understand it. The wise man knows that life too is beyond his understanding; but he knows what life is and he can accept it. Hamlet's divagations about life and death are not at all important as truths about life and death; their importance lies in the revelation of character, a type of character which symbolizes the absurdity of philosophy divorced from action. The trinity which epitomizes Hamlet's behavior is composed of guilt, doubt and fear. This is the death trinity and it is on this trinity that the whole superstructure of man's thought-world has been erected. It is the tribute, if you like, which death exacts of life. It is life's nourishment, for life springs from death just as much as death from life.

In a type like Hamlet, whom I suppose you would call dead-alive, the emphasis is not on what he is, but on what he is not. You talk of yourself in the same negative way. I think that even the common man understands this very well. If he fails to be intrigued by the problems you pose it is not because he is incapable of following you, it is because he is indifferent to you. It is true, he is indifferent to a great many things, but that is the nature of the common man. That is a fact which has to be accepted, like death. No matter how fantastic a man's ideas may be he can always gain adherents if he himself believes in his idea passionately. The idea may be death itself, but the passionate belief in it is life. The whole Elizabethan drama is saturated with the death theme, and we all know what life there was in it for the Elizabethans. The whole history of Egypt revolves around the cult of the dead, and the Egyptians we know were vitally alive. What is wrong with your death theme? It is because you are not talking about death, but about pseudo-death. A man cannot give us the account of his pseudo-death and appeal to any but the pseudo-dead. To bring your philosophy over into life, to move living people, to strike death and terror into the weak and cowardly, you have to talk real death. You have to believe in mortality and immortality. You have to be a contradiction in essence, not in theory. If you are for the death of an outlived tradition, as you say, you have to be passionate about that and prove to us that it really is dead for you by living deeds. You have to put the vitality of your revolt against this living corpse into your books; you cannot fight a corpse with a corpse. And that is what you are trying to do.

You say, look at me, how dead I am! and thus you hope to vanquish the other living corpses about you. My dear fellow, you've got to really go dead on them, otherwise it's just playacting. In Hamlet this playacting has serious consequences eventually; the same may prove true in your case. But the end of Hamlet is nullity, as was the beginning. I take it that is not your goal. It take it that, unfortunately, you want to get somewhere. Watch out that you don't get there too fast! Take a cue from the Orientals whom you cite: sink into contemplation, arrest the mental processes. Cultivate blankness of mind, as the Chinese sage suggests.

19

January 26, 1938

So you think I have been taking unfair advantage of you so long?
I wish it were as simple as all that. You see, it may be easy and
convenient to use two signatures, to live two lives, to write poetry
and to sell books—*easy for you*— but to others it is quite confusing.
You are not clearly divided down the middle, like those illustrations
in anatomy books. When one looks at you he doesn't see two people,
and even the two signatures, when they are compared, will appear
to come from the same hand and the same brain. I am not trying
to quibble here, believe me, since this is the very heart and bone of
the schizophrenic problem. And you are not yet a schizophrenic—
but only schizoid, please remember. True, there is a valid distinction
between the tendency and the malady itself. You are *aware* of the
split, but that does not also say that you have brought about the
necessary fusion. Rather, it seems to me, you hug to the split. Just
the other day, in reading about Goethe again, about his spiritual
evolution as revealed through *Faust*, I came across this utterance of
Jacob Boehme's: *"Who dies not before he dies is ruined when he dies."*
Here we have the acceptance of duality and of death in life. The
death is even regarded as necessity—certainly not as a disease. They
get the impression of a blur, which is vulgar language they have
many unpleasant terms for, but all of which signify lack of integrity.
Lack of integrity can become a virtue when raised to the highest
degree, as exemplified by the (mythical) person of Lao-Tse. And
integrity can come to mean something quite different from what is
usually associated with the term, when we consider the life and

sayings of such a (mythical) person as Jesus Christ. Both these individuals, legendary though they may be, brought about a terrific confusion through their utter clarity. They were human absolutes who polarized two permanently conflicting trends in the human psyche. In each of them the force of example was so great that, in my opinion, we were obliged to make them legendary, mythical. I believe that is entirely possible for two such individuals to have lived, thought and acted as they did. I also believe that it is incredible for them to have done so. I believe that the men "of the record" existed, but that the record part is ours, we who would like to believe in them, their deeds, their utterances. I do not believe that they were absolute, in life. But I do believe that the absolute was so strong that the relative, human side of them has been forgotten. At bottom I have no objection to such a procedure on the part of the human race; it is all part and parcel of the creative instinct. We retain that which we wish to retain of a man; it is the part which corresponds to the man's own inspiration. And it is in this sense that I guard my image of you, deformed, caricatured, unfair as it may seem to you. When, for example, instead of confining myself throughout this book to our subject, dear Hamlet, when instead I speak of you, of you as Hamlet, I am not deliberately striving to malign you. I am taking the subject as it strikes me, or, if you will, as it pleases me. Everything I say about Hamlet and you is absolutely true, even if it sounds crazy. In fact, the more crazy it sounds, the more true it is apt to be. It is the way I understand and feel Hamlet. Had I elected to write the book with Durrell, for example, an entirely different sort of correspondence would undoubtedly have ensued. Does that mean I have other conceptions of Hamlet? Why yes, a thousand different conceptions, all of them true and sincere. In a way I am very happy I chose to write this book with you. However personal it may seem to you, to me it seems like the most impersonal thing imaginable. This makes you think I have no core, and a lot of other nonsense. The thing is that I keep my core well inside me where it belongs. I never worry about the apple not being all core. Everything has a core, and when one is split one has two cores. And that is where people of your temperament create difficulties for yourselves; you divert attention to the tension between the two cores, instead of the core itself. At the extreme limit, when what is called reality seems to have disappeared, there are a thousand cores; in fact, the personality is nothing but a grand network of little embryonic cores, each capable of developing into a single individual. But the core itself is never destroyed, not even in the wildest reaches of schizophrenia. That is why you are perfectly right in not fearing the phenomenon. It is not new, as I said before. In fact, if you push it far off, you can read God as symbol for schizophrenia. He is the utmost awareness of his multiple selves, secure in the awareness, and able to sit out an eternity to recover his wholeness.

And now I may bring a smile to your lips, but again I repeat that I am absolutely sincere when I say this: we must all help God to come into his own. We must help the world! Jesus, if you want to look at it in another fashion, you might say it reminds you of that Western Union messenger boy who wrote me saying that he prayed to God every day in order to help make the company a success. Yes, it is that way. And the moment one realizes that the only way to help the world along is by being utterly one's self, by being alone and unique, then one ceases to worry about the external pattern, the rise and fall of civilizations, or this or that temporary social or economic or political order. One has the chance at every moment to become a unity and to embrace the whole world, the good with the bad. It is no longer a question of code, or ethics or morality, no longer a question of the right or wrong viewpoint, or of the long or the short of it. Becoming empty, in the old Chinese sense, means (as here above) to strip yourself of all views and all cloying personal attachments. You become less humane, perhaps, but more human. You become a being instead of a personality. You don't need a signature even: you subscribe to nothing and to everything. You go through a *real* death in life, which is what makes the other death, when it comes, truly fructifying. And it is the real death which, as I hinted before, you have never gone through. The double signature is the evidence of a *double life*. A Siamese soul life in the one body. You were not born with two souls. You were not created a freak. (Parenthetically, I have seen so-called freaks in the side show who were the very essence of integrity. I knew a few of them quite well at one time— particularly, I remember, a lady without legs. But that's another story.) I only mention it perhaps because that idiot St. Augustine was so preoccupied with freaks and what would happen to them after death. But he was *literally* preoccupied—there wasn't the vestige of symbolism in his arrant nonsense. And you, when you talk sometimes about the "man of the record," or about dead-alive, remind me of St. Augustine. I put you in the same category, because you are both "men of ideas," obsessed by ideas. You even say you *are* an idea, which would not be at all shocking if we accepted it as a tribute to the creative force in all of us, but no, with you it goes beyond that, it becomes literal, it becomes not a whit different than the literal hocus-pocus of Annie Besant and all that theosophical crew. You are taken in by the idea, instead of exploiting the idea. It is the old business of identification again, the fear that unless you become as the thing itself you will never possess it. It is really a sophisticated form of voodooism, as I see it. And Plato, whom you so much admire, is one of the most flagrant of these voodoo worshipers. But Plato I leave to one side, for the moment.

I don't mean to say by all this that you are exceptional in your duality and duplicity: it is the norm. And when anything is rigorously examined it appears quite monstrous. And the normal is a monstrous thing, if it is regarded frankly. But that is only to say that human life itself is a monstrous affair. In the sight of God, that is. In the sight of God the normal is the abnormal. Nothing must horrify God more, assuming He could be horrified, than the sight of the normal man. And if you want to smile again, you may smile now when I say that it is the God in you, the man striving for perfection and for absolutism, which is horrified by the weak human being in you, the other abominable everyday self which has to transact the dirty business in order, as he wrongfully imagines, to keep alive. It is this fear of not being able to keep alive which permits and encourages us to condone the evil in ourselves, or if you don't like the word evil, then the petty, picayune self.

Any man who has become so thoroughly aware of his dual nature as you have must admit that this characteristic was produced at some moment in his life, that it had a source and origin of a painful nature. I don't think I am exposing your private life unduly when I ask you to admit this. Most of us go through this at one time or another:

I mean go through an experience which is unbearable. But it is just because we refused to go through it utterly that we become as we do; we know that nothing is too terrible to face. Men have voluntarily elected to face far worse torture than you (or) will probably ever know. They were not terrified! They accepted the ordeal voluntarily, sustained by the illusion, perhaps, that they would thereby undergo a marvelous unknown experience—a rebirth, usually. The stake and the rack will never disappear, you may be sure of it. Nor the cross, which is the most profound symbol of man's life on earth, of his struggle with his own nature. They will disappear only when birth itself ceases to be a phenomenon of nature. For man, whether erroneously or not—I think erroneously—has got it in his head that birth is painful, that birth *is* a sort of death. Which it is, of course. But has any one proved to us that death is a painful thing, a bad thing? Though I had no chance to welcome my own birth I can and do welcome my own death. Any kind of death. Most of what is called life I know nothing about, and I do not worry about these things nor fear them. Why should I worry about or fear my own death? And if I am only half-alive now, I don't worry about that either. It is the part of me which is alive that interests me and keeps me going: the dead part will take care of itself, with time. Time is with me, that is what I feel absolutely. I have nothing to lose, or gain, in time. In time everything is O.K., and that is where I situate myself. What bothers me are little problems, like the next meal, the next book, and so forth. Not metaphysical problems. Not any question of my own identify, my own desires, my own longings. I have only physical, biological problems. You don't seem to believe that. When I say I am hungry you talk about my soul or about my lack of loyalty. Whereas all I ask is a little food, *real* food. (Or, if not you, in certain instances, then others. It is a common failing not to hear rightly when a man asks for simple things like bread and money. People get strangely metaphysical then, you may have noticed). And, in a profound way, they are right of course, even though it hurts me to say it. When people turn a deaf ear to a simple plea for help, they are doing what I have just done a moment ago, in referring to your illness. They are trying to point the way back to the source and origin of the trouble. The difference in my case is that I believe in helping first, and pointing afterwards—sometimes I even refrain from pointing at all, believe it or not. If I point, it is with a clear conscience, that is with the same guilty conscience as the sufferer, having been there myself, having befuddled the issue, having gone a-begging, and having died miserably by the wayside, through neglect and desperation. Hamlet Prime would not have gotten a word of consolation from me, it is true. Nor do you, our modern Hamlet, seem to get much consolation from me. Only death can close out the account between us. While you live you are on my books as a human entity, a flesh and blood creature, say a friend, if you like, and withal a damned queer specimen of a man, but a man, by Jesus, and not an ideological rat in the entrails. And with a man I am apt to make mistakes, apt to do the wrong thing now and then, apt to praise him too much, apt to betray him too. I am not dealing in logarithms, but in human values, human relationships. It is a wrestling both in which there is a lot of love and a lot of hate, though most of us are loath to confess the hate part. And this book, which was really an act of friendship and of mutual esteem, just because it is a creative, malleable, plastic thing, can sometimes take on a distorted quality and appear like a piece of analysis. But it is not that, and I don't see why you should fear it. It is a positive act of revelation, set in motion by our mutual awareness of common bond: Hamlet. And Hamlet again is not for me X, Y, or Z, though it may be as you say a good excuse to talk about X, Y and Z. No, Hamlet is Hamlet to me, something very definite, even in its tenuousness. It has color, weight, quality, substance. It is not the ideological rat-trap business. And just because it is a live thing, having flesh and substance, as I say, it will never, no matter what course it takes, sever my relations with you, never make you more of an enemy or more of a friend than you now are. Hamlet is a subject to me, or the symbol of a subject which has manifold aspects, and which will not be resolved or talked or written away by this, our book, or any other book. Hamlet is part of the time stream, just as the Revolution is, or Lao-Tse, or Jesus H. Christ. Hamlet is a permanent part of the human psyche, a gleaming facet of which Shakespeare gave us, but which he did not exhaust nor dispose of. And I don't think you either hope to dispose of the subject, though you may try to dispose of me *en passant*. Just as the drama of Christ which we must all live out was crystallized in the miracle of Golgotha, so the Hamlet drama will be crystallized again and again in the course of time. Hamlet is the drama of man's inner duality, the drama of his swerving allegiance, his irresolution. It will not be disposed of: each man can at best live it through, make what he will of it for good or ill.

I tell you often that, in my opinion, nothing much is to be hoped for from the present species of man, the Homo Sapiens type. He is only a stepping stone to a higher type, or perhaps a lower type. If the world is our creation, as I firmly believe it to be, one can see that the drama which we are playing out—which we have been enacting ever since the Flood—can end only with the dissolution of us as type men. The problems which invest us are problems of our own creation entirely. I refer naturally to the spiritual problems. We make no real progress, no real evolution: we oscillate from one pole to the other. But within this seemingly closed frame, this prison which we have constructed for ourselves, a few men have arisen from time to time who point the way to an entirely new kind of life on earth. They had the power, it would seem, to set up mighty currents, to change the external pattern of our lives, so alter the very face of the earth—but they were not able to create the new type which would live out the hope which they inspired. They exist as pointers, as weathercocks, if you like. No more. They stood out as men who were against destiny. They drew up their own private horoscopes, established their own private destiny, and that is the most important thing about them. They were non-historical figures. The language which they employed is baffling to us. Nobody can decipher the truth behind their utterances because this truth was embedded in their actual life. Wrote out their own prescriptions for their own private illnesses. They were unsocial and anarchic—and beyond all that sublimely indifferent to the fate of others. By their own example they seemed to predict another way of life which to us would appear as sheer insanity. They dreamed of a world without protection, without security other than the inner security. This sense of solid security which emanated from them has become our refuge, our protection. We eat them alive in order to obtain a precious bit

148 / HENRY MILLER'S

of security for ourselves. We are all in the wrong track, savages still in all that relates to fundamental things. Usually in such crises a man admits to his own shortcomings, to his own failure. When a man feels neglected or abandoned or misunderstood or underestimated he usually discovers that there is something wrong with himself. You take the stand the world *ought* to come to you, *ought* to seek you out. Nietzsche went mad waiting for the world to come to him— and he deserved to go mad. Others greater than Nietzsche have not had this problem: they so acted that it was impossible for the world to ignore them. In Tibet the great lamas actually makes it difficult to be reached; instead of encouraging their disciples they put obstacles in their way, so that finally the disciple realizes that he has no need of the master. The Hindu crowd is different from all other crowds in the world, so it is sad. It is a crowd composed of self-centered individuals: each man is concerned about himself, about his own salvation. "The sad thing about the world," says a Chinese philosopher, "is that the things which ought to happen do not happen, and that the things which should not have happened do happen." I myself do not believe that anything *ought* to happen: what happens is just, I believe. I no longer blame anybody for anything. I accept full responsibility for everything that happens to me, whether it is just or unjust. There are plenty of things which are beyond my control, but what is not beyond my control is my ability to accept or not accept. When the way is easy I forge ahead; when it is too difficult I sit back and let things take their course. There are things I can do and other things I cannot do; I waste no time trying to do the impossible. Nor do I waste energy fighting or hating. I seek to reach my level, that is all. My life is a creation; that others have a part in it I do not deny, but it is my own part of it which interests me and concerns me. There is no "ought" involved; *there is*, that's all. Why do I act? Because I like, because I desire. I do all I can to make my life the way it suits me. The satisfaction is inner, not outer. In a crude way I see everything that happens to me taking place as I wished it. The astonishing thing is not what does *not* happen, but how much happens that one did not expect to happen. Ten years, twenty years, thirty years later something is produced which was once ardently desired; one hardly recognizes the materialization of his deep wish. But it happens! It almost seems like a law, and indeed that is what Amiel so often stresses, that what one wishes for occurs, that what one desires one becomes. And if the world is in a state of confusion, of distress, of disagreement, who can deny that that corresponds to the living desire of millions and millions of people now existent? One wants too many things which do not belong to him, so many things which he has not earned or is not willing to earn. It is not just that there should be a terrific confusion, a terrific disorder? Consider the wealthy Hindu who gives up all his possessions, his family ties, his position, and goes out into the world as a beggar. (It happens every day, I suppose you know.) What a relief that must be, to strip oneself naked and take up the little begging bowl! Is he crazy, such a man? Was St. Francis crazy, or Buddha, or Christ? What happens to world problems when a man really isolates himself from the world, from his fellow men, in deciding upon such a course? We know that the contrary is more apt to be the case, that in depossessing himself of all ties he unites himself to the world by inseverable bonds.

Is this the shadowy bond with the world? You see the phrase "to earn a living"—you see it as a reproach sometimes, as though to say, don't you too have to earn a living? But it seems to me that this is evasive on your part, to put such a question. It does not really concern me how you earn a living, how any man earns his living. That is *your* problem. Yes, I too try to earn a living though I have not yet succeeded, and I am already in middle age. It is quite possible I shall never earn an honest living. Perhaps I don't truly care enough whether I do or not. Perhaps other things occupy me more. But when I do beg, borrow, steal or prostitute myself, in order to earn a living, I don't set up an alter ego on which to shove the blame. I admit that it was I, Henry Miller, who did the lying, the thieving, the cajoling, the this or that, whatever it may be. I can look back upon my actions and deplore them, I can develop a certain amount of guilt about them, but I don't deny them. On the contrary, I exploit them, I use them to build up my whole self more solidly. I know in my heart that one makes progress with only the least part of one's self. One must go forward on all fours, accepting the punishments as well as the rewards. One is crucified not for the sins he commits, but for the lapses, the discrepancies. One is crucified for not being a one hundred percent God which he is. And that is just, it seems to me. The duality of man is his cross; if he would eliminate the corpse, eliminate suffering, he must eliminate the duality. He must become more of an animal and more of a God, at the same time. He must work forwards and backwards in the present. If he wants to remain a social being he must accept the mask. But he can't talk about integrity and sign two signatures also. That is like the criminal who says society is to blame. Certainly society is partly to blame; but each man has also himself to blame. Focusing on society gets one nowhere. Society is the composite of millions of men living together, millions of separate entities each working out his own salvation, his own creation. There is as much of me in society as there is of society in me. As I change the world changes, imperceptible though it may be. Sounds Emersonian, I know, but no matter. I am convinced of the truth of it. Society is not changing in any haphazard, whimsical manner. Society changes daily according as we change, each and every one of us.

And now to talk about myself a little more intimately I will tell you how I feel about the future—*my future*. Every day I live in three times—the past, the present and the future. The past is the springboard, the present the melting pot, and the future the delectation. I participate in all three simultaneously. For instance, when I write something I like extra well I smack my lips and look over my own shoulder. I am already with the man of 2500 A.D. or 5000 A.D., enjoying this great guy Henry Miller who lived in the 20th century. There are certain things I do which while doing them I know beforehand will be appreciated later on. I am sure of it— dead sure. I gloat over the past, I revel in the present and I make merry in the future. What it takes the ordinary man a number of incarnations—supposing there are such things—to live out, I live out in a lifetime. I have the accelerated rhythm which goes with genius. I make no bones about it—it's a fact. I am gay inside all the time, even when I am depressed. I never doubt for a minute. Never. I am dead certain of everything. I do not even sign contracts with my publisher any more. What for? What have I to fear, what have I to lose? I am inexhaustible. And to date nobody has ever yet done me a dirty turn. Nobody has ever cheated me, that I can say. Now and then I may do a little cheating myself—but as for the others, no, not one ever does me a dirty turn. The longer I live the less protection I demand. As I explained it to Reichel one night, if you are an artist, that means that you are denuding yourself more and more, that by the time you die you are stark naked and your bowels turned inside out. If you are an artist it is quite legitimate to talk about "the man of the record," because there is no other man and there is nothing but the record. Everything is gravy to you and everything turns back into gravy—it slops over and runs right out into the backyard. I feel very happy about the bad times we are living through and always have lived through. I am glad to be a maggot in the corpse which is the world. I feast on death. The more death there is the stronger I become. Bigger, fatter corpses, is what I say! I am on my way to Godhood, a little angel worm now, but eating my way through and leaving no dirt behind. I am helping the world along with my fine digestive apparatus. Sometimes I begin to munch before the corpse is cold. A friend is talking to me, for example, and not realizing that he has not yet turned cold, I begin to bite into him. You should try that some time. It's like eating cold turkey with a hot sauce.

Anyway, this is the point. Somewhere you talk about words, words, words. I say fine! Words are never just words, even when they seem just words. For the hand that writes there is the mind that reads, the soul that deciphers. Some write syllabically, some cabalistically, some esoterically, some epigrammatically, some just ooze out like fat cabbages or weeds. I write without thought or let. I take down the dictation, as it were. If there are flaws and contradictions they iron themselves out eventually. If I am wrong today I am right tomorrow. Writing is not a game played according to rules. Writing is a compulsive, and delectable thing. Writing is its own reward. *The men of 2500 A.D. will enjoy reading this little passage, I am sure.* for, don't forget it, there will be Fraenkels and Millers then as now, and there will be the same debate, the same problems, only different. I know when I am giving the man of the future pleasure; I share the pleasure with him in advance. You don't settle anything; I don't settle anything. Everything remains unsettled forever, depend on it.

But when we say something by which they recognize us that brings pleasure. I tell you, I feel very close to the man of the future. It doesn't matter to me whether the West declines to the point of death and extinction or not. In the same West there will be men who understand what I am saying and who approve, no matter what the fashion may be, no matter who the emperor may be. I pity the emperor as I pity the slave under him. I know they will both enjoy my work, regardless of their circumstance or position in life. I wonder do you ever feel that way about the future?

20

Sitting on the edge of a volcano to finish this duet I am working with my bags packed and my hat on my head. At the first sound of the siren I blow. I don't want to participate in the conflict nor to be a spectator. Since the events of the last few weeks I feel more than ever separated from the rest of mankind. Their worries are not my worries, their aims are not my aims, their solutions are not my solutions. Perhaps the most impressive and at the same time the most depressing sight I ever witnessed in my whole life was the mobilization here in France. The grim, silent, unrebelious, unostentatious way in which one citizen after another dropped out of the ranks of the workaday world in order to reappear a few hours later fully equipped and part of the death battalion struck me with horror. In 1927, living in America, the call to arms was not precisely a death warrant; there were things one could do at the last moment, there was even a chance to rebel and go to a concentration camp, if one preferred. No European has this chance today, and worse, he does not even dream of the possibility of availing himself of it. Not even the most sensitive, cultured individual dreams of refusing to take up arms: it is no longer a law which operates, but an instinct seemingly. That is to say, they are all trapped—high or low, rich and poor alike. The country comes first, no doubt about it. And the best types are the ones who will be bumped off first—that's also indubitable.

I must go back a bit to explain more fully the revulsion I felt. Some time ago I saw an American film, the title of which I forget, which gave me a cold chill, which terrified me and disgusted me more than anything I have ever seen in the movies. The story had to do with the efforts of the English authorities to stop the slave traffic. It revolves about the trial of a man who had wantonly, cold-bloodedly murdered a number of men, women and children. (Yes, now I recall the title: "Murder on the High Seas.") The hero, who had been entrusted with a most important document, which was supposed to bring about the cessation of the slave traffic, finds himself aboard a boat on the high seas which is floundering. He is flung into a small boat in a semiconscious condition. He comes to find that the boat is overcrowded and that a huge mast which has fallen athwart and it threatens the lives of all who are in the boat. In a moment, and without a second's reflection, he is on his feet throwing people overboard right and left regardless of age, sex or condition. Some of them attempt to swim back to the boat, whereupon he gets out his revolver and shoots them; those who have succeeded in getting hold of the boat he goes at with a knife and chops off their hands. In another few moments he has completely cowered the survivors and taken command of the boat. The mast is removed and the oars are manned—and of course he succeeds in bringing the survivors to port and surrendering the most valuable document which is to preserve the lives of thousands of innocent blacks. The question which arises is—is this man a hero or monster? By his quick thinking, his sense of reality, his *action*, not only the lives of thousands of black people have been saved, but also the lives of those in the small boat which would have gone down had it not been for his presence of mind. I say that the man was a monster and that no matter what beneficent results his action entailed he had no right to murder those whom he did. I say finally that it is not even certain that the results of his action were beneficent. Asked what I would have done in such a quandry I replied—"I would never have found myself in such a position." I think it is clear enough what I mean. The situation one finds oneself in is always the situation one has created: we are always at the point or place we desired to be. The man of action always finds himself in the thick of the melee, obliged to kill without thought, without let. To prevent murder he dies murdering.

Not long ago I was reading an essay on "Hamlet" from Maeterlinck's *Wisdom and Destiny*, an early work, I believe. He asks the reader to imagine what Christ would have done in Hamlet's position. It is a suggestion which is unthinkable, unthinkable mainly because it mocks the supreme intelligence of a Christ. I mention this apropos of the situation in which we, the supposedly intelligent people of the world today, find ourselves. I am not even thinking of the immediate situation, the crisis through which we have just passed and which we shall undoubtedly have to meet soon again. I am thinking of the way of life which the so-called civilized man has adopted for the past few thousand years, which promises to continue with minor variations for another few thousand years, or perhaps for a million years to come, who knows? I want to confess that under the strain of the last few weeks, threatened by a destruction such as no sane man hardly dares to imagine, I was profoundly shaken and finally, after an inner conflict such as I have not known since I was a lad of twenty-one, came to the conclusion that my earliest judgments were confirmed, and not only that which might be regarded as a triumph of vanity, but that chastened, subdued, hardened by the test, I must continue to assert what I believe is true and best—at least for myself. Perhaps a great deal lies in the phrase "for myself," for more than ever I came to realize in these last few weeks that I have no counsel to give to others, that I have no solution to offer the world—but that I do know better than ever what I myself should do and want to do. I could not help thinking also during this trial of the genesis of this book in which we are collaborating, of how from a reckless indifference to the title and subject matter (because we were so confident that we could not possibly miss the crying problems of our time) I for my part, at least, have found once again that the problems are not world-problems situated outside the self, but *the self*. I want to confess that today at the age of 47 I am nearer to where I was at 21 than I have ever been, and that I am glad of it. I mean to say that at the age of twenty-one I was nearer to being "on the path" than I have been at any time since. I had chosen then what is called an "unworldly" life, to which, because of my deficiencies of character I was unable to adhere. Today I have chosen a "worldly" life, in the fullest sense of the term. The world of experience which lies in between has served to weld and fuse what appears to many as opposites. Today I believe that it is possible to be in the world and of it and at the same time beyond it, an attitude which was impossible for me at the age of twenty-one because I did not know the world, because at that time I was intent on *altering* the world, and that in the most ineffective way possible, by a straight-lined, idealistic attitude. Today I am hardly an idealist, nor even a realist, but a confirmed dreamer who accepts the unreal as a solid unshakable fact. Today I believe absolutely that everything about us, our world, our behavior, the skies, the climate, the forms of life, we ourselves, are a creation, that we have the power to create life as we desire it, and that all criticism, all reproach, should be directed against ourselves and ourselves only. Today I assume full responsibility for what I am and where I am. And as I have just been through a second Hell I can assure you that what I say I say most solemnly.

And here is where I feel compelled to resume the subject of "responsibility." For if there is any one on God's earth who has had luck, who has escaped "miraculously" time and again from the snares and pitfalls created by his own ignorance, his own transgressions, it is myself. I have tempted Fate right up to the last ditch. When finally I righted myself—some few years after landing in Paris—I understood clearly the pattern of my life in the past and resolved inwardly to alter it. And just when it seemed that I had come to a full accord with my destiny, just when I felt that I was master of my destiny and not a mere puppet, came the threat of universal destruction. The threat is still there, and indeed it looms larger than ever, more inexorable than ever, but I no longer react to it as I did before. No matter what happens, I feel that I have won a tremendous victory. I want to explain what I mean . . .

In anchoring myself here in the Villa Seurat these last four years I was unconsciously identifying a state of inner peace with the place which reflected my aura. Until that place was threatened vividly I was unaware of what I had done. In the crisis I felt that my own inner peace was threatened, which it never was. That peace I won to by hard effort; it was a peace achieved through desire, and not a blessing of the gods. It was perhaps the first true condition of the self which I had ever earned. When I abandoned the sanctuary, so to speak, I experienced the feeling of one who has been cut adrift. In the past, whatever ties I had were physical or sentimental; I was never tied to possessions, but I had been tied to individuals, to relationships. This time I was tied to something far deeper, to a creation, which I had unwittingly concretized. I was attached to the ambience of a state of mind which was the first real, enduring creation I credit myself with achieving. The Villa Seurat became identified with all France, with her destiny. You can imagine my anguish. Today the Villa Seurat no longer exists; it is a waystation, another lap on the road to fulfillment. For me the war which was so narrowly averted really took place; I have relinquished my place and my possessions once again. I resume my life, as the majority of men will perhaps only twenty-five or fifty years later, not at the place where I left off, but on an absolutely new terrain, at a beyond which was unthinkable to me a few weeks ago. The problems of that period are obliterated, forgotten already, solved, as most problems are solved, by a new *modus vivendi*. And this is a little more difficult to explain, because man seldom recognizes the true nature of his problems until long after they have disappeared. Perhaps it is just because the problems are so very real that we appear to be so inadequate. Always, it seems to me, it is the one problem, the problem of REALITY. Always, it seems to me, it is the question of the *decalage* between our desires and our behaviour. It is as simple and bald, I might almost say, as the matter of "integrity." This problem, which is wholly individual, admits of no external solution.

Before leaving Paris a month or so ago I managed to finish the first volume of Capricorn—"On the Ovarian Trolley." There are some curious pages in this book, as you will soon see—pages which leaped right out of my Unconscious. There are long passages which were written from word to word, line to line without the least premeditation, I, the writer being as much amazed as the reader will be when he sees them. Time and again I harked back to a period in my twenties when I first began to write—or tried to write. I spoke of how, in that trying period when to write even one line seemed a herculean task, I had the distinct impression of being closer to the Australian Bushman or the Igorode or the Hottentot than to my friends and compatriots. I felt that the most "backward" of men would understand me better than my American neighbors. Further, often when I was put to it and obliged to leave the house in search of fodder I would think not only of my wife and child who were waiting for me to return with arms full but of these same primitive beings scattered throughout the world: I would think of them and their plight, wonder how they were getting along. I used to marvel that there could exist millions of men in the world concerning whom we, the so-called civilized beings, never gave a thought. I tell you all this to amplify a conviction which seized me during the last few days of the crisis. As we were sliding rapidly towards the brink the question which often arose in my mind was—has man always played into the hands of Fate or is there really an opportunity to surpass himself each time a great problem arises? It seemed so clear that the supposed problem was altogether secondary, a mere pretext for a show of strength, for a showdown, as we say. It also seemed very clear that if it came to the final issue, war, nothing would be solved, but instead we would be faced with new and perhaps more insuperable problems after the war. What enraged me and sickened me throughout the negotiations was the unwillingness on both sides to make real concessions. I saw that the people around me were in dread of what might happen, that their real desire was for peace at any price. And yet, when the moment came and the first mobilization was announced, there was not a dissenting voice: the summons to arms was obeyed as though it were the voice of God commanding them. I saw with my own eyes and with the most profound sadness what I have always known to be the truth about humanity in general—that between their real desires and their actions there is a gulf as wide as hell itself. I saw that millions of men were ready to sacrifice their lives, their homes, their families by going to war and not one man ready to sacrifice his life by *not* going to war! I said a moment ago that the real desire of the people was for peace, and that I think was amply demonstrated by the jubilation with which the Accord of Munich was greeted. But this desire, which is a tremendous force and which has never been exploited by the statesmen, is only the negative aspect of a will which is bent on destruction. The peaceful instinct in man, the Western man, at any rate, is still merely an expression of his selfishness, his egotism. He does not want to be harmed or molested—but he has never once made the resolution that, come what may, he himself will never harm, never molest another. If he had the courage *not* to defend himself against the aggressor peace might become a fact, a reality. I'll speak for myself, give you my own reactions and reflections...

In the past I often used to wonder why it was that the horrors of war never profoundly altered man's consciousness. It is not enough, for example, to say that man forgets too easily. Forgetting is just as active and willed as remembering. At Bordeaux the day after "peace" had been announced I saw the cardplayers going back to their card games. (Every one went back to his accustomed groove—to my amazement and astonishment.) But the cardplayers chiefly interested me. They played right through the crisis and when the crisis had passed they continued just as before, as though nothing had happened. For the most part they were the oldish ones, those who were well-off and had nothing to do in life except to kill time. Many of them doubtless shared the sentiment of my dentist who said to me during a critical moment: "If anything goes wrong with that tooth just come back here—*I'll* be here, no matter what happens, it's my assistant who will go to the front," and so saying he turned to his assistant and gave him a smile which I shall never forget as long as I live. Later, when I was alone with the young assistant, a lad of twenty-two or so, he said to me—not bitterly, not reproachfully, mind you, but calmly and resignedly: "It's not very funny for me: I will be in the first line—it's sure death."

To return to the other side of the fence, to those who pretend to themselves that peace is a desirable order of things, to those who are always ready to sacrifice their lives for the maintenance of the status quo. The cardplayers are a superb symbol for these individuals. They are old and weary, they have sufficient with which to "get by," they are indifferent to the sufferings of those around them, they ask only to be left alone and in peace. That's the real aspect of the situation today, and even a child can understand it. And even a child, if its mind is not already blunted by education, might understand that the cardplayers are equally guilty before God, that war is brought about through a desire to be left in peace as much as by a desire to expand and conquer.

Well, you begin to get the drift—how life goes on in its accustomed way up till the last horn, how not even the threat of universal extinction can change human behavior. The man who exacts his pound of flesh in peace time exacts it at the end too. The beggar remains a beggar before and after. The cardplayers play while Rome burns. The police stand in readiness to arrest the thief and the burglar. The dentist's assistant drops his drill and goes quietly to the front to be drilled with holes. If Christ suddenly appeared in the sky, *in person*, and said in his clear gentle voice—"Peace be with you!" the mobilization would go on just the same, the bombers would attack, the woman would collect her eight sous, the clocks would strike the hour and the terraces would still be crowded with people sipping their aperitifs. Christ himself could come down and butt his head against a tree and nothing would be altered. I think perhaps I would be the sole idiot who would stand up and recognize him and salute him. And for that I'd probably be put in a strait-jacket.

I think of Nijinsky, of that diary they dug up not so long ago, of his saying: "I am not an ordinary man. I love God and He loves me. I *want everybody to be like myself*. I am not a spiritualist, not a medium. I am a man in God. I am afraid of perfection because I am afraid people will not understand me. My life is a sacrifice because I do not live like others . . ." That he was stark mad when he wrote the diary makes no difference whatever to me. He was just mad enough to write the most poignantly truthful, naked words that we have seen in a long time. *"I want everybody to be like myself!"* The French publishers and editors laugh at a phrase like that. He was crazy, the poor devil! they say. The book doesn't interest them—I tried it on a number of them.

I mention this phrase of Nijinsky because in the days that followed the "accord" I felt very much as he felt when he was writing the diary. I too felt that I wanted everybody to be like myself. I felt that I was completely alone, and I was not terrified but sad. Above all, I knew that I was not mad. I never saw so clearly. I tried not to judge, but I could not help weighing the scales. My intelligence told me one thing, my heart another. If I must sacrifice one of them it is my intelligence I will throw overboard. I want to live by the heart, which is the real seat of intelligence. If my intellect tells me that life is unbearable I will discard all that I know and learn all over again to accept life and to love it. At present I am still moving about in Hell. I see nothing but evil and ugliness about me. I see the results, the effects, of all past behavior. I see the realism of the French as a shoddy intellectual compromise with life. I see all Europe as a world sound asleep and thrashing about in a nightmare. I see beyond Europe, and nowhere do I see a people awake, moving about in Reality. Deadlock. Complete deadlock. But the forces which make the world are not null and void. The forces of life are working all the time, silently, underneath. We are all part of those forces; what the humblest man does also counts. And what one does not do counts too! In some cases counts heavily.

People will tell you that I lost my head during the crisis. I don't deny it. I am glad I lost my head! I want to throw my head away every time—every time, I mean, that keeping one's head leads to putting it in a noose. A friend of mine, an older man, told me before leaving Paris that he would not mind doing his bit again (he would not be up front this time, anyway!)—he said he had always enjoyed soldiering. Another friend, a very young man, wrote me that he didn't care what happened—it was good too to sacrifice one's life *for nothing!* Another friend informed me that he would continue to work away at the Bibliotheque peacefully, right up to the end—which he did, I must say. For every man there was a different reaction. Perhaps the men I sympathized most with were those whose opinions were not asked for, those who are counted upon to drop their tools and go without a word. In the movies later, seeing a worker kissing his wife good-bye at the station—no drama, no sob stuff, no heroism, just grim acceptance, fate, fatality, French realism: that was like putting a spike through me. An old woman with an infant in her arms standing before a kiosk reading the mobilization order: her mute face was eloquent, unforgettable. Every one sees it differently, reacts differently. Catastrophe has a million different ways of recording itself. War is not just war: it is a universe which each one explores to a different end. Myself, I am terrified of it. If this is cowardice, then I am the vilest coward of any man on earth. As long as I have two legs to run with I shall run from it, and if necessary, I shall crawl away on all fours, on my stomach even, wriggling through mud, anyway, anyhow, but out of it! Even if what I see about me now is Hell, it is Life just the same, and I prefer this life of hell to the gamble of war. I love life above truth, above honor, above friends, country, God or anything. I want to keep alive until I have had enough. I want to die of my own desire, peacefully, fulfilled, in bed if possible, and in my sleep. I don't want to be overtaken by death—I want to summon it when I am ready. I believe this is within my power, and further, that it is my prerogtive *as a man*. A man who tells me he "enjoys soldiering" is not a man, in my opinion. A man who is ready to sacrifice his life for nothing does not know yet what life has to offer. A man who says that this life which we have on our hands now is the only possible life, under the circumstances, is a traitor to the human race. A man who wants to defend the status quo by arming tooth and nail is the murderer of that which is living and beautiful and true. In 1917, when I was twenty-five, I didn't have a moment's hesitation about deciding what I would do. I knew instantly war was declared that I would not go. This time I wavered. I was enmeshed, and worse, I was enmeshed by my own creation. I had created for myself a good life, a life which suited me. I was at one with myself. I wanted to preserve that achievement. But as I have related, I realized in time that there was nothing to be preserved by fighting. The enemy of my peace was not merely the Germans but those at my elbow too, those everywhere in the world who are ready to defend the status quo. My real enemy is organized society. *I want everybody to be like myself*—in spirit at least. I am not an enemy of *man*: I am an enemy of stupidity, bigotry, patriotism, injustice, selfishness, callousness. I don't need to kill anybody to establish my way. I can assert myself even under the conqueror's heel. I can live my life even as a slave. I am certain I should always be the master, no matter how ignominious the relationship. I don't care for the appearance of things, for the epithets or sobriquets; I care only about the reality, and in reality I am at home. If, for example, I were permitted to stay here at the Villa Seurat (supposing the war broke out tomorrow), if I stayed on and the Germans were victorious, if they marched in and took possession of the city lock, stock and barrel, if they were quartered here in this house, the lords and masters, so to speak, do you think that I could not get along with them, much as I despise and detest them? Certainly I could! I could get along with a Kaffir or a Hottentot. I even wager that I would be quickly appreciated, esteemed by the enemy. If they asked me to shine their boots and wash their dirty dishes, to scrub the floor and run the errands, do you suppose I would take it badly? Not on your life! I would do the same for the Communists or any other tribe of fanatics who happened to take possession of the world. And if they asked me to salute in their fashion, to swear by their oaths, even if they asked me to goose-step, I would do it, by Jesus! I would do it gracefully—until I could find a way to slip out of their clutches. *But if the whole world starts to goose-step*, I can hear you exclaiming—*what then?* My dear fellow, I can assure that that day will never come. There will always be a square foot of soil somewhere on earth which the enemy either cannot conquer or does not consider worth conquering. *There* I will entrench myself, if I can make the getaway. And if it be necessary to kill a few men in getting there, to dirk them in the dark, I will do it with a clean heart. I am not ashamed to murder a man, if it is necessary, but I am ashamed to go to war, to murder in cold-blood and for a cause which is not mine.

I go back to the room early, thinking perhaps to write a bit. I haven't opened the typewriter since leaving Paris. As I undo the valise there on top lies Erich Gutkind's book: *The Absolute Collective*. It is the only book I have brought along. I lay it on the table together with the toothbrush and razor blades. In turning round I see hanging over my bed a crucifix! I can't tell you what a rage that put in me. I had half a mind to rip it off and throw it out the window. There I am with this wonderful Jewish book in my hands and the crucifix staring down at me. How am I going to sleep in this room? That thing will give me the willies. I take it down and hide it in the little night table with the pisspot. *That* for your sickly-looking Jesus, thinks I to myself. Outside it is pitch dark and the mountain stream is making a torrential noise, like a high-powered dynamo going full speed. I open the balcony window and step outside to take in the view which the proprietress recommended to me. The illuminated cross is blazing still; in the garden below are the palmtrees; the air is chill, colder than Paris.

I go back to the little table and write a few lines in the little book. "I am in the lowest sphere of Hell . . ." The crucifix is lying in the pisspot. Outside the door two maids are sitting on a bench: what they are waiting for Christ only knows. It seems like a sanctimonious bordello. Maybe it's a private whorehouse for the priests, who knows? Anyway, it's freezing, and I think the palmtrees are responsible for it. I go to bed in despair. Nature surrounds me: the Pyrenees, the Basilica, the palmtrees, the bazaars, the crutches that were cast off. I toss about. It seems that a strange odor emanates from the room. I can't make out what it is. I lie there thinking of the strange place it is that I have chosen for a little peace and quiet. I am chock full of energy, nervous, fidgety, wide-awake. I begin to picture in my mind other visitors lying in this bed. I see them coming, in droves, like cattle, during the holy season, the open season for miracles. I see them coming in wheelchairs, on crutches, in ambulances, in private cars. They are all sick, twisted, deformed, disease-ridden. I see them coming on like an epidemic, wave after wave, each with his own special brand of disease or deformity. They seem like microbes personified, microbes raised to the human power. Suddenly a feeling of horror comes over me. That smell! Yes, I know now what it is. It's DISEASE. The room is full of the germs of the dead and diseased. They have left their maladies here, their black souls, their sins, their crimes, their cancres, their pox, their benighted brains. The room is crawling with evil spirits. They swarm over me like lice. They are hidden away like bedbugs in the wallpaper. Whew! but the place is foul, foul with the Catholic legacy of God. I fall asleep finally, to dream that I am a huge jellyfish buried in a cake of ice.

Here I am, I thought, eight years in France, and just as much of an alien as ever. I thought of the few French friends I know and I wondered how they would react to this atmosphere. Finally I began to think that this wasn't a French atmosphere at all, but a sort of universal protozoic slime of man in his lowest denomination out of which all peoples, all races, struggle more or less ineffectually to create an "atmosphere" which is livable for the truly human spirit.

I wondered where Balzac had written his *Seraphita*: I thought of Giono living among the degenerate remnants of the Mediterranean peoples and creating there, in a solitude almost frightening his grandiose dreams of the natural man. I remember the emotions I experienced when I returned to America on a visit and stood before the little old house which had meant so much to me as a child. In front of that house I wept—*for myself!* I wept to think that a life I might have known had I been born in some other part of the world. Perhaps I would never have written a line—but does that matter? I would have known a better, richer life—that is what I believe. For some of us too much of one's life is wasted in liberating oneself from the hideous thralls of environment. As far as character goes it may be worth while to undergo these trials and tribulations— but it is not ultimately essential in the development of the human spirit. I *knew* that as a boy I was equal to the best that life has to offer. I *know* that from manhood on I was obliged to make a detour which was not absolutely necessary. I am only now coming back to that point in the road where I switched off many years ago. I may be absolutely wrong in what I say, but that is how I feel. And when I stood before Fenelon's statue in Perigueux I almost wept with joy; I don't know his life but I feel almost certain that he must have stayed in this spot all his life. And even if he did not, I am certain that he never deserted it in spirit. And how fortunate he was, in his hours of mediation and reflection, to be able to walk through the crooked, picturesque streets of the old quarter! For us who are born in America the old quarters have ugly memories; we have no connection even with the men who founded the country. We are more hostile to them in spirit than the peoples they fled from. No root takes hold. Life builds up on succeeding levels of fossil, each level revealing an epoch separate and distinct from the other. And at the bottom, instead of the solid core of earth, is quicksand and quagmire in which the historical and the biological alike will perish without trace.

There are writers, too, and perhaps they are among the greatest, for whom "place" has no significance; one feels that their books may have been written anywhere. With them environment is like the clothes one wears, not a whit more noticeable in their works than clothes are when one is confronted with a great soul. Others, on the other hand, and they also include some of the very great, seem to reveal nothing of themselves or of their struggles, but only the atmosphere of place. For me the place and the thought are always associated: either I create the place or the place creates me. In the most solitary flights I am always aware of *where* I am, as I am also aware of the hour, almost to the minute. I never think of a beyond as an escape or refuge but always as something here and now which will be transformed—and transformed through my active agency. I never crave the impossible, but only the marvelous which, from experience, I know is right at hand accessible at any moment. It is in that sense that, like Nijinsky, I wish everybody to be like myself, in the sense that they might be privileged to experience the wonders which I myself have already experienced. The date and place of these experiences have a certain value for me, much as the markings of a channel have for a pilot. If tomorrow, for instance, I should go again to Toulouse and meet with an altogether different experience that is not to negate my previous experience. Toulouse, like every other place, is a universe—and I am a universe too. And there are times when these two universes meet in transit and establish a grand conjunction, as it is called in astronomic parlance.

When I came to Paris in 1930 I had this feeling of a "grand conjunction" very strongly. I should never have endured what I did during those first years had not this sense of a mysterious significance, of destiny, been strong in me. Today I no longer feel that it is "necessary" for me to stay here; I feel that I am moving along in a current of forces, as yet undecipherable, which are leading me to another *significant* halting place. I feel that the problems— social, cultural, political, spiritual—which occupy the French today have no importance for me whatever. I am almost like the Jew in my resistance to assimilation. I don't *want* to be assimilated by any people: I want to fecundate! The more individualistic one becomes the less places there are to go to, naturally. One is considered more and more as a traitor. And one *is* a traitor, no mistake about it, as long as one is not resigned to the frozen flux. And one is even more the traitor if one refuses to preach revolt. The whole world today is in revolt against something or other—but no one is in revolt against himself.>

All of which leads me back to the endless duel over the Hamlet theme, to the question of surrender to the stagnant flux or liquidation and readjustment on a higher, more vital level, a level in which we are opened up. I can never see anything more in the Hamlet tragedy than an inferior drama of sacrifice. To me Hamlet always represents the supreme coward who walks out on LIFE. Nothing is solved by his action: the results is murder and suicide. Hamlet does not surrender, nor does he grow wiser, nor does he open up. He brings the drama to an end by killing off the players, himself included. For a paralytic action means disaster. The paralytic suffers from a congestion of the will; his will is atrophied because it is isolated in the trinity of bodily harmony. The will usurps its prerogative. A prisoner of his own making, there is no escape, no solution possible except by blowing up the prison. In history we see whole peoples coming to this impasse and repeating the disastrous experience. In the Greek dramas, in the best ones, this question of Fate revolves about the conflict of man and gods. The poet describes the defeat, or humanization, of the gods; actually, if we look at the situation historically, it is man who is defeated. The poet remains locked outside the historical pattern; he is the eye of God which illuminates the drama but is powerless to alter it. And yet the truth of his vision persists—and operates. Whole peoples, races, nations, go down, empires crumble, ideologies fall apart, cycles commence and recommence, but the vision of the poet remains and inspires and nothing goes forward until the others come abreast of the vision. Athens won out over Sparta, only to crumble later because the vision could not be sustained. Defeat comes with the loss of integrity, and the impending death always manifests itself through the survival of will which, once an expression of unification, in the end becomes an instrument of destruction. You may have noticed, incidentally, that the French have never used the word Will as the Nordic peoples have; but they are coming around to it now, for at last the death throes are on them. They are the last European people to lose their organic unity; they cannot preserve it any more because they have lost faith in it themselves. The body is crumbling and organs and limbs are being fast replaced by mechanical devices which will obey the blind switchboard of the will. All the colonial expansions and acquisitions of the European nations, the great artificial respirators, are breaking down. Even the supreme Will is powerless to maintain their efficacy. With the collapse of the lungs, even the best scientific lungs, the heart stops beating. An implosion occurs which drives the collapsed organisms to the surface of reality there to be picked by the scavengers of the new order. Underneath another life is preparing, another human world composed of the same substantial ingredients. The dead matter on which the scavengers feed becomes transformed. There is no repetition: there is an absolutely new experience each time. The earth is changing with our changes. Every death quickens the earth, makes it more alive, more real.

Similarly, it seems to me, the dreams of the idiots today and for the last hundred years or so, will also be realized in the centuries to come. That dream is of economic independence, and I have no doubt it will be achieved, though perhaps in a way and through a form of life wholly unexpected. I believe that the Machine will be incarnated and will dominate man's life in dual fashion, as he has allowed himself to be dominated in the past by other ideas. I believe it will take centuries yet for man to pierce the fallacy of the machine way of life. I believe there will even be a certain amount of good resulting from his life with the machine, but ultimately it will be discarded—because it has no place in reality. The subservience to the machine seems to me almost like the last lesson for the narrow, restricted personal view of life which man has. The world will really become the Hell which the machine, as a surrogate form of life, symbolizes. Man will come face to face with himself and see himself as a substitute for the real thing. He will have to surrender his narrow conception of life, his unreal desire for security and peace, for a protection from without, a protection wholly artificial and created out of fear. He will have to learn to live, not only with others, but with himself. He will discover that his comfortable world of economic bliss and security is in reality a straitjacket. He will see that he is surrounded by useless appendages to himself, the concrete manifestations and crystallizations of his own fears. The machine will become a myth as the Avenging Furies of the Greeks have become myth for us. Nothing can prevent this long and tedious experiment, for this is the real desire which is at the root of our present-day conflicts. It doesn't matter what ideal or ideology is proclaimed, in what name men fight and die: what is real and what will be made manifest is this desire for economic security. They will have it, the men to come, and they will wrestle with the evil which is bound up in this specious blessing. There will be men a thousand or two thousand years hence who, in their frantic desire to preserve the status quo, the era of economic bliss, will point to us of today as an example of the horrible condition from which they escaped and into which they are in danger of relapsing. But they will not relapse back into our condition of things. They will relapse forward; they will fall back blindly on the invisible wave which carries the human race on from round to round of ever-increasing reality. They will be carried forward as dead matter, as the debris and detritus of a vanished order. The Hamlet dilemma, which today we call neurosis, seems to me to be a symbolic expression or manifestation of man's plight when caught between the turn of the tides. There comes a moment when action and inaction seem alike futile, when the heart is black and empty and to consult it yields nothing. At such moments those who have lived by illusion find themselves high and dry, thrown up on the shore like the wrack of the sea, there to disintegrate and be swallowed up by the elemental forces. Whole worlds can go to bits like that, living out what you would call a "biological death," a death which Gutkind calls the *Mamser* world of unreality and confusion, the ghostly world of Hamlet, the *Avitchi* of the Buddhists, which is none other than a world "of effects." Here the unreal world of ideas, dogmas, superstitions, hopes, illusions flounders in one continuous nightmare—a reality more vivid than anything known in life because life had been nothing but a long evasion, a sleep. Hamlet's fear of the other world is the most real thing about his philosophizing. For him nothing could be more certain than that he would toss fitfully about in hell. He represents a lost soul, in that he could neither decide to go to the right or to the left. He is left high and dry on the far shore with the tide running out. He is doomed to live among the ghosts of his own creation, doomed to be forever dispersed as a living entity, to recommence, if ever, as the lowest elemental substance.

In a way, and you may laugh at this, the drama of *Hamlet* seems to me strangely linked with Shakespeare's own surrender and dissolution. In a period of feverish activity, when life was running strong, as we say, the man who is the crowning product of the age, who leaves his stamp on it forever, unleashes one drama after another of fury and despair. By other peoples Shakespeare is always regarded as an elemental force, as a sort of blind embodiment of chaos. The rugged common sense which has been distilled from his mad lines is at variance with the poetic despair and impotence which makes his creation so enigmatic. Nothing is built up architecturally, as with Dante; there is nothing epic about him, as with Homer. He stands in the midst of his works like a shackled, tortured giant, casting a pitiless eye about him. His illuminations are terrifying: they reveal a world of lies, confusion, cowardice, treachery, disillusionment, aborted love, murder, greed, in short, the *Mamser* world which lies hidden behind the cloak of the ideal. Shakespeare was unable to accept the reality of that other world which he knew; he felt the tide running out under his feet, and though he was a Colossus he was unable to move, unable to acknowledge the sway of the supreme force which expresses itself in flux and reflux. For English-speaking peoples he seems like the incarnation of a world, the summation almost of all their hopes and dreams. I do not share that feeling. I know small, isolated, almost unknown words by so-called lesser men, which for me put the whole of Shakespeare's toppling edifice into the pale. I do not worship force or energy as such. A Colossus can be impressive *and* meaningless. An insect sometimes can teach me more than a man. And a flower still more. I am not *against* Shakespeare so much as indifferent, untouched. *Hamlet* intrigues me, and will always intrigue me, because I am at a loss to understand the hold it has over others. I understand *Hamlet* only as I understand the bankruptcy of a whole people, a whole culture.

The loneliness of the modern man, which is so poignantly foreshadowed in *Hamlet*, bespeaks an emptiness which is the very opposite of the condition of a sage who achieves aloneness. This latter state the Chinese express by a word which signifies "alive-and-empty." It corresponds, to my way of thinking, with Buddha's idea of "annihilation," which has nothing to do with extinction but rather with an expansion of the self to the uttermost limits. The hell of loneliness, which in Buddhistic language is called *Avitchi*, implies selfishness and consequently separation. But there is no integration or expansion possible simply by falling back into the collective life; the man who relapses to a lower sphere of being, because of loneliness, because he is not understood, experiences the tortures of hell. No man is alone who is thoroughly himself. An advance does not mean a break but an enrichment. To enter into a new and more vital realm of experience means liberation with the old thralls. There is no "sacrifice" for the man who follows his vision. Those who remain behind interpret it as sacrifice: it is easier for them to describe things negatively than positively. The "renunciation" which every great man accepts has nothing negative in it; on the contrary, it is the expression of a positive choice, an earnest of increasing freedom. It is a relinquishing of the shackles which fetter. In the Hamlet type, which is the modern man par excellence, we see instead a surrender to the forces which bind and imprison him, we see him refusing to make a choice. For every humiliating and ignominious defeat which he suffers he advances the reason that he could not do otherwise. He expects the world to be altered in order that he may adjust himself to it. He behaves as though he were something apart from the world, a creature privileged to enjoy an immunity which is unknown to other creatures of Nature. He prefers to see his neighbor altered rather than alter himself. He craves a life compatible with his ideal; he never thinks of idealizing his own life. The end is sacrifice to the flux which knows nothing of the "ideal." The whole world is now in arms over questions of "ideal." The ideals will perish with those who hold them. The ideal has nothing to do with reality: the ideal simply implies the survival of a vicarious mode of life.

In my own short life I've experienced the two tidal impulses: I've known evolution and involution, and stalemate and paralysis, and despair and ecstasy. What I thought was courage I've seen later was cowardice, and vice versa. I've had to learn to distinguish between hope and desire, between prayer and communion. Every time I finish a book I realize that nothing is finished, that the book is not important but writing itself, and not even writing, but expression, which can be on any plane. When I speak of ceding everything to the enemy I am thinking not only of pride, possessions, place, prestige, but all the evidence of creation. I don't wish to be attached to anything I've created any more than to a home, a country, an idea, or a memory. The act was important, not the product of the act. To become more and more creative is to become more and more detached, free, flexible, alive. To become fully alive. To become fully alive, to burst with life, that is my goal. Anything which must be defended is a fetter, only arrests the flow. No situation can be ✓ ignominious if one is detached.

I've been aware of the operation of a strange law these last few years. It is this, that if one refrains from hoping, praying, yearning, one's desires are realized or gratified almost immediately. It is almost as though the wishing and praying for a thing to happen deflects one from the target. Everything is realized in due time, and time itself seems like a bridge which we construct to reach a goal which we overlook because it is right under our nose. The difficulties we encounter arise largely because we fasten on an end, because the moment we are pregnant we expect the child to be delivered. The healthy mother goes right on doing her chores until the last minute; she doesn't waste her strength and courage thinking about the delivery. The modern mother thinks about the pain and the discomfort, worries whether the child will be normal or abnormal, wonders whether she will die or not, and so on. And the result is frequently an abortion, an idiot, or a Caesarian operation—or else death. And that's the way the political-minded individuals behave. They are concentrating on the ends they hope to achieve. They all describe a glorious future for their respective countrymen, but to attain the bliss which they so glibly promise us we must first wade through rivers of blood. I don't want any dam constructed for my benefit, even if it promises an inexhaustible reservoir of power. In fact I don't want power: I want to *feel* power everywhere in all things. When a man hoards up power like a dynamo he must discharge it some time. The dynamo is a mechanical device which doesn't interest me in the least. Any man who wishes to convert himself into a human dynamo is for my part welcome to do so— I don't envy him. I feel that I have all the power I need; I replenish myself from day to day out of the common storehouse of energy which is available to every one free of charge. When I see people cramming themselves with knowledge, or trying to stuff themselves with right feeling, I pity them. Hamlet, for example, was a learned fellow, full of good intentions, a noble soul, as they say, and yet an absolute imbecile, a failure, a murderer and a suicide. I see people now and then who go in for occultism, in the hope of tapping the secret of life, or discovering "the way," the path to fulfillment. Every more they make is off the path. They want to possess something, a key, if you like, to penetrate the mystery. But the man who stands before the mystery has never provided himself with a key; the man who recognizes the mystery takes care to veil it again. He lives *in* the mystery and practices occultism openly.

When I left off yesterday I made a note to write you about the garbage can, about the necessity of living close to the garbage can. It is strange how, when your mind is thoroughly occupied with a subject, everything you see or do seems to have relation to the subject, to confirm and corroborate your ideas. Filled with thoughts of the virtues contained in the garbage can I went to the Cinema des Agriculteurs to see the Yiddish film, "Green Fields." The drama, as you probably know, revolves about the conflict in the heart of an overserious rabbinical student between the spiritual (here revealed as the orthodox Jewish attitude of the priestly class) and the purely human attitude. The role of the serious young student "in search of the truth" (sic!) is admirably played. He seems to go through life in a trance, his eyes so obstinately fixed on "the truth" that he is blind to what goes on about him. He never employs his limbs to any useful purpose; he is gauche, shy, ignorant of everything except the teachings of the Bible. The peasants with whom he is staying during his pilgrimage quarrel with one another for possession of him; they treat him like a fatted calf, nourishing him so well and rendering him so useless that finally his eyes are opened. Finally he realizes that God not only desires a man to know the Sacred Scriptures but to work with his hands too. The author shows him slowly succumbing to the wholly human life of the common man, the man who tills the soil, who earns his daily bread by the sweat of his brow.

I give you the theme crudely as you are probably only too familiar with it. I have even been tactless enough in the past to point out to you the danger of such a conflict, as exemplified by your own behavior. Often, when you are at your best, your "noblest," I have sensed something ridiculous about your attitude. I am not going into that again, as I have no desire to make fun of you personally, or to criticize you justly or unjustly. I merely wish to point out that the poet, or angel, cannot go forward at the expense of the *man*. If one does not recognize the "bright" and the "dark" sides as parts of phases of the whole, then one is doomed to swing back and forth perpetually like a pendulum. One has got to get above and beyond the opposites, to take his stance in the Absolute in order to live out a life of *relative* freedom. The Absolute I refer to, is not the Absolute of the rabbinical-minded, but life.

I come back to the garbage can which for me is a vivid symbol of what I mean. In the course of a day I am obliged to go frequently to the garbage can. As you know, I not only do my own marketing but I cook my own food and wash my own dishes and scrub my own floor—and I handle my own garbage. There are people who pretend that they have more important things to do, they couldn't be bothered with all these menial tasks, they say. I find, on the contrary, that it is no bother at all, that in truth it is refreshing, stimulating, illuminating to perform these drudging tasks. How often, in handling the garbage have I received the most illuminating flashes! How often in washing the greasy dishes or cleaning out the sink have I mediated well and profitable! I might say in all seriousness that I am often nearer to God when doing the dirty chores than when listening to Bach or Mozart. So many writers seem to imagine that in order to write a good or a beautiful book they should refrain as much as possible from coming in contact with the sordid, the mean, the ugly things of life. They think that to turn their back on evil is to put themselves face to face with the good. They ignore the laws of transformation and permutation. The man who tills the soil is much nearer to understanding the process though he is often powerless to make use of it. But the "higher" types are usually hopelessly shut off from this wisdom. Hamlet again is an example of the removed thinker who is cut off, better—who has cut himself off—from human affairs, from life. Who ever thinks of Hamlet as possessing a body? Hamlet is pure mind, a dynamo of thought whirring in the void. He never stooped to put his hand in the garbage can. He is the Prince of Idleness, an addict of thought and futile speculation.

It seems to me that there are indeed two very real form of detachment observable in man, the one wherein the individual is exclusively preoccupied with his own development, and the other wherein the individual's very real development brings about detachment automatically. But this latter is only a seeming detachment; actually his type of individual, because of his quickened rhythm, gives an accelerated impetus and elan to those who have not yet come abreast of the vision. His actions are not drowned or lost in the stream of human activity, but only temporarily unnoticed, because the vibrations are of another wavelength. There are men, in the former category, who attain to the highest levels—and who are lost to the world forever. They were obedient to the one impulse only, and when that impulse exhausts itself, when the tide turns, they are left stranded, matters little. They remain forever out of communication with the world. It was only in re-reading what I have written you just recently that I became aware of the great error I myself made in saying that I preferred life above everything. In speaking of life that way I was guilty of making it Life with a capital L. That is to say, of making it the all, of shutting out its twin, death. When a Buddha, for example, stops at the threshold of Nirvana, when he renounces the highest bliss, the merging with the all, his action illustrates for us the paradox that acceptance and renunciation are one and the same. Flux and reflux, for this highest type of man, are the same as life-and-death for the ordinary man. There is no separating them out. The desire for *life* is an admission of the fear of death, the recognition of death, the vulnerability to death. I admit my error. Indeed, I was aware of this error when I wrote my preface to *Bastard Death*. I saw it in you, because you had raised Death to pre-eminence. You had introduced Death with a capital D. But I was not aware of making the same mistake myself by swinging into a feeling for Life with a capital L. This is not mere logic which I am giving you, please believe me. This is something I feel and know. To make it real is the most difficult thing I know of. I write about it frequently, either directly or obliquely, but acting it out requires the fullest, most constant awareness. One gets caught by a desire for truth or goodness or beauty, just as any idiot gets caught in his low passions and vices, just as the thinker gets caught in his passion for knowledge, for solutions, just as the analyst gets caught in his extremely human role of healer. In the assumption of any role, even the highest, even that which is on the side of Life, one surrenders to death. The role of the Exemplar, which is admittedly the highest, is also identified with death, and causes death as well as life. I say that, because I put the Exemplar above the Teacher, who is very obviously arresting life by the very act of teaching. But even he who forbears to teach, who adopts the role of the Master, through action, even he is capitulating to death in so doing. There is no true teaching except by example, admitted; but so also is there no healing, even if one sacrifices his life to the good of humanity. Life should not be sacrificed, even for the highest principles, even for the good of the world. When a Buddha renounces Nirvana it is not a sacrifice of life! HIs act constitutes a reconciliation between life and death; it is the last manifestation of choice, and though, according to the doctrine, the Buddha is no longer chained to the human wheel of birth and death, his spirit remains *this side*, as a leaven, as an invisible influence as quickener. Whether you believe in the doctrine or not is immaterial to me. I don't believe in it myself altogether. I think the doctrine, all doctrine, is negligible. I think that every Buddha that ever lived was essentially against doctrine; I think he was even against the power of his own example, as example. Whatever he was, he was unique, and example is therefore vain and futile. The man who is uniquely himself has no need of a Buddha or a God. This is a flat pronouncement, and I leave it for you to demolish it with zest and vigor. Every man who is uniquely himself comes face to face eventually with the true dragon, which is the Self, and which must be slain in order to make the final reconciliation. This supreme acceptance, of life as a life-and-death process, saves one for the world eternally. One doesn't escape to a beyond, or become dissolved in the All: one liquidates—to flux what is flux and flux what is reflux. One embraces the Sun *and* the Moon.

Coming home in the Metro today I observed a distinguished looking blind man enter with a woman who was apparently his wife. They sat opposite each other, he busying himself with a mechanical contrivance for rolling a cigarette and she watching him sadly, shaking her head from side to side as though to say "dear me, dear me!" The contrast between them was impressive; he seemed calm, possessed, perfectly at ease, a man who had evidently been something in the world before losing his sight; he even disdained to carry the white cane, or to take her arm; he made the minimum of groping gestures, judging his position and relation to the things about him with remarkable nicety. She, on the other hand, seemed hopelessly muddled, lost, despondent, wasting her substance on pity and regret. I had the feeling that if some one had said to him, "I will give you your choice: to have your sight restored and be this woman, or remain as you are," that he would have chosen the latter. In fact, I will go further and say that he gave me the distinct impression of having gained something by the loss of his sight, and that he realized it himself. The woman was very obviously thinking of all that her dear husband was missing by not having his sight, whereas he, it was clear, was contentedly profiting by all that he had gained through his loss of sight. One felt that the world had become richer for him through his deprivation; in accepting his loss he had been compensated by a deeper sense of reality. One almost envied him, so marvelously was all this shown on his face. The wife who was pitying his plight was the one who was really blind; she saw only the cigarette machine, the tobacco pouch, the subtle groping gestures; she did not seem to see the light which radiated form his countenance.

There are other cases where the blind, as we read about occasionally, suddenly have their sight restored. I speak of those who have been blind from birth, or from early infancy. And what do they tell us, these people, when their eyes are unsealed? That the world is ugly, that human beings are ugly. I remember one case where a young woman admitted that if she had known what it would be like she would have preferred to remain blind. What a commentary upon our vision! For what we see every day with our physical sight is but the image of the world which we carry inside us; our whole creation, this world about in which we live and *have our being(?)*, corresponds to the inner vision. Everybody participates in the creation of the world; no one is exempt from the curse of the enshrouding gloom, the ugliness, the villainy. The man who lights up the tiniest corner of the world with a clear vision and a pure heart kindles a flame which all the forces of darkness are unable to extinguish. This steady, quiet glow of the visionary, this beacon light, outshines the light of the great collective swarm of fireflies who flutter about in the dark. Nothing can stand up against the light, not even the dead moon which hangs in the sky like a reminder of this truth. At night, when it would seem that the great visionary had withdrawn his radiance, the whole firmament is alive with countless other visionaries, all testifying to the eternal presence of light. How strange and perhaps maddening it would be if they drew closer to us, these brilliant worlds of light! We are not yet ready to receive such a brilliance, such vision. We would wither in the brilliance of such a light, for what is alive in us is feeble and demands the dark protection of the body.

But sometimes through the blind we get a glimpse of the unquenchable fire from whose source we all obtain the light; we realize that our feeble physical sight is but an intimation of the human beings are more than they seem, that they contain within great nourishing vision which sustains life. We know then that themselves limitless universes, just as the sky. We see that when ordinary vision is deprived from the eternal vision lights up, that in losing what seemed so precious they gained new vistas and more splendid ones. Blindness is voluntary and it is only the *choice* of the individual which should elicit our compassion—not the plight itself. For even the worst plight contains the seed of regeneration, of transformation. Nothing is lost, except for those who have surrendered, who have relinquished choice.

You may have noticed how, when you make ready to leave a place which you have outgrown, suddenly, in the last look about the place which had once been so alive has gone dead, dead beyond all hope of resuscitation. One looks at friends and lovers too that way sometimes. And finally I suppose one can look at the whole world that way—but without sadness or regret. When you experience this deeply the last thing on earth to come to your mind would be to wish it different. The detachment, when it comes about through growth, is comforting and sustaining. One feels that he is already to another world—alone for a short time until he gets his bearings. *But the more one is truly alone the less lonely one gets.* The dead worlds are like empty vessels and who would want to live in the empty vessels? Being alone is being alive in the fullest vessel, the profound life in the symbol, which is inexhaustible. Those who have mistaken the form for the substance go on living the empty life of the empty vessel; they are crowded together in the void, and no matter how many they are or how tightly squeezed together, they never make *one*. This life which they know is life in death, which is endless decomposition and ramification, numbers, decimals, fractions— never a single, solitary entity. They not only smoke dream cigars and drink dream whisky but they die dream deaths. They never really get buried because there are only dream undertakers. The dead bury the dead, as the Bible says. But this sort of dream life, dream death, dream burial goes on all the time, endlessly, hand in hand with real life, real death, real burial. It is not peculiarly characteristic of certain epochs; it is only that at certain periods in man's history, whenever there is a great new collective life preparing itself, man becomes conscious of the death racket. Those who are ready to die with the spent wave make use of this death language in order to identify themselves, as individuals, with the new form of life ahead. When I say "collective" I don't mean some autochthonous, a new form of life which manifests itself from the roots up.

There is a thought which comes to mind every time I touch on the death theme and that is the ghostly character of violence. The killing that men have indulged in continuously has a ghastly quality of unreqlity. Hamlet is a marvelous example of the fear-ridden egomaniac, not a whit different, for being a poet, than Tamerlane or Caesar or Hitler or any American gangster: the lust for power, the desire to avenge, are like the struggles of a foetus in the womb. And when the conflict becomes worldwide and we see whole peoples ranged in deadly combat the spectacle takes on such an unreal character as to be hallucinating. "The human world," says Gutkind, "is the world that is fully alive." And the transition from the womb-like prison which we know to the human world in which we are fully alive and no longer kill is as simple as to open a door and step out. This has been demonstrated to us time and again by great individuals: it involves nothing more than choice and will. The whole network of conflicts in which one is enmeshed, seemingly hopelessly, is sloughed off like a dead skin. But, as I have said time and again, the solution is too simple for most people to grasp. People are always trying to force the locked door; the forget that they have the key in their pockets. And they forget because the terror of opening the door into a new and unknown world is too great. One prefers to get adjusted to killing and being killed, to fighting shadows and creating systems which are of no value—*unless one does not consider himself a hopeless prisoner.* The whole of human activity often seems to me nothing more than the pastime of convicts in the death-house waiting for the hour of execution. Sometimes the whole creative activity of man seems to me nothing more than a swansong, and it *is* in so far as it is restricted to art and not to the personality. Every advance in the realm of art reawakens this terror which slumbers in the breast of the doomed—that perhaps art has to do with life, that perhaps art is nothing more than a means to greater life. And when a man comes along who has emancipated himself from art he is regarded as a madman and quickly put under lock and key or else crucified or else sanctified, which amounts to the same thing. I said recently to some one that I intended to stop writing at the height of my power—not as a whimsical or defiant gesture, but as proof of the realization that art is only a means of revelation. I feel already, at times, that I have no further need to write another line; I need perhaps to go on writing until I am absolutely sure of it. But the idea is there, latent, and I am sure that it is based on a truth. And if I kept the silence it would not be to revert to a lesser manifestation of life, such as the world of action offers. I would not be giving up art because it had proved ineffectual; I would put the significance which art reveals into living. I would close one door to open another. It would be converting words into silence: acts rather than action. I mean to say by all this that the renunciation would betoken an even greater confidence in life: it would not be a retreat but an advance. For most artists this realization is practically coincident with death. That is why, in attempting to unravel their lives, one is obliged to go to their work, for the man lies entombed in his work. some, like Rimbaud, who renounced their role of artist midway did not advance but regressed; these men are even more enigmatic to us than those who covered themselves with oblivion through their monumental labors, for it is difficult to separate in them that which belonged to life and that which belonged to death. They did not renounce, I ought to say, *they surrendered*. And though they seemed to have abdicated in favor of life it is to death that they really made their abdication. And dying of their own volition, in the very midst of life, they have never been properly buried, and they never will be: they will stick up above the engulfing sands, like the enigmatic Sphinx, mysterious, unreadable, the very incarnation of the riddle of life.

What I have to say in this book will probably be finished before the war breaks out. This evening, in the movies, I saw a news reel abut the Maginot Line, intended, I suppose, to reassure the good citizens of France that their country is well defended. I can imagine nothing less assuring, nothing more depressing, nothing more significant of despair and hopelessness than the Crazy Maginot-Siegfried Lines. To see the genius of the two greatest nations in Europe symbolized by the erection of two parallel lines which are impregnable is like reading the word BANKRUPTCY written into the soil. While their respective emissaries of peace and goodwill fly over these impassable barriers to sign their names to new pacts of non-aggression the military chiefs, with the aid of their devilish technicians, work like beavers to make their respective lines more impregnable. What greater expression of supreme doubt could there be than this spectacle which is being offered us? Can any sane man believe in a pact which is made by two bandits armed to the teeth? Did hope and despair ever reach such extremes as this? Millions of people all over the world will undoubtedly see this news reel sooner or later. The effect? nullity. Nobody will do anything different after seeing the picture than before. And yet the picture says very clearly: *This is how and where you end!* The peace pacts are mirages: reality is centered in the Maginot-Siegfried Lines, in all those complicated means of destruction which are hidden away in the earth there where the two great peoples of Europe confront each other and are unable to meet and mingle freely and openly. Only a little distance either side of the lines are the cemeteries where the last bloody mingling took place. In the interval one pact after another has been solemnly signed and flagrantly broken. Another generation is about to go up in smoke and flames. Meanwhile, the recreation, we pay to sit in a cinema and study the intimate details of our threatened destruction. This is called "progress." This is how civilization marches on. As for myself, I read everything backwards. Behind every assurance I read doubt, behind every hope despair. I can't separate the men who are running the machine from the machine itself. I refuse to believe anything connected with this mechanism, whether it be called defense or destruction. I see only fear and doubt everywhere in everything. And so I write you these closing pages with a most solemn realization of the debacle which is impending. I realize that I shall have to carry on somewhere else and in a manner wholly different from perhaps any that I may have anticipated. Most of the intelligent people with whom I am in touch are not intelligent enough, I must confess, to rearrange their lives in view of the reality which stares us in the face. They are still dreaming of carrying on from behind the lines, still hoping and playing, I suppose, that some last minute change of heart will occur. Much as I would welcome any change of heart I am positive that it cannot come about. The human race is not the sort that brings itself to the point of destruction in order to experience a change of heart. Peoples, like individuals, dig their own graves. The death which infects the earth is simply the record of error and defeat. The whole planet can go dead, dead as the moon, if the race continues in its present course. The sky is brilliant with blazing worlds of light, but we of the earth seem to be following the fate of the new extinct planets. No matter what happens here life will go on, but through our folly and ignorance the show may have to be transferred to another sphere. With all my power and intelligence I intend to keep myself free to carry on the experiment elsewhere, if needs be. I shall do my utmost not to die before my time, and especially not to die in the preservation of a condition of life which is false and unworthy of man. I do not know yet what course of action to pursue, but I am meditating on it, and I have no doubt that the way will be revealed to me. I believe in aiding Fate, not tempting it. *I believe that when one has life he will know how to guard it.*

—Henry Miller

MICHAEL HARGRAVES was born on February 29, 1952, at Jacksonville, Florida. He was introduced to the writings of Henry Miller while attending the University of Florida, where he earned a B.S. in broadcast journalism/cinema in 1974. He has authored various works (listed below) and has also written short fiction as well as catalogued several major collections of rare books and photographs. He is currently at work on a novel entitled *Threading Needles*.

BOOKS BY MICHAEL HARGRAVES

Henry Miller Bibliography With Discography (1980)

Triple-Decker Kiosk (poetry) (1981)

Harry Crews: A First Bibliography (1981)

The Hamlet Additions: The Unpublishing of The Henry Miller-Michael
    Fraenkel book of Correspondence called HAMLET (1981)

Times, Things Change (poetry) (1983)

Eight Obscure Literary Autographs (1983)

Harry Crews: A Bibliography (Rev. ed.) (1986)

Robert Gover: A Descriptive Bibliography (1987)

AS PUBLISHER

Ishmaelite Scrolls by Benjamin Barry Hollander(1979)

The Cagliostro Arcane by Jack Hirschman (1981)

Bring Me The Head of Rona Barrett by Robert Gover (1981)

A Chapter from Blind Tongues by Sterling Watson (1983)

Tropico, the City Beautiful. Photos by Edward Weston (facsimile ed.) (1986)

SCREENPLAYS

Kiki of Montparnasse (with Frederick Kohner) (1977)

Confusion (with Jacques Tati) (1978)

The Man Who Thought He Was Groucho (Based upon the novel *Madder
    Music* by Peter De Vries) (1980)

Overkill (1982)

Love In The Ruins (Based upon the novel by Walker Percy) (1983)

Murder City (Based upon the novel by Oakley Hall) (1984)

Coming Into Focus (1985)

Restaurant: The Motion Picture (1988)

tergiversation — to become a renegade apostatize

virago — strong, willful, courageous woman.

hagiography — a glowing portrayal

eschatology — study of Last Times